A DESKTOP REFERENCE MANUAL OF COMPLIANCE TERMS

A DESKTOP REFERENCE MANUAL OF COMPLIANCE TERMS

◆

Regulatory Compliance Associates, Inc.

◆

Bankers Publishing Company
Rolling Meadows, Illinois

THE CONTENTS OF THIS BOOK SHOULD NOT BE CONSTRUED AS LEGAL ADVICE. READERS SHOULD NOT ACT UPON INFORMATION PRESENTED IN THIS PUBLICATION WITHOUT INDIVIDUAL PROFESSIONAL COUNSELING AND CONSIDERATION OF FUTURE DEVELOPMENTS.

Printed in the United States of America

No. 560 ISBN 1-55520-135-0

ACKNOWLEDGEMENTS

This publication represents the work of many. Not only have all the associates at Regulatory Compliance Associates, Inc. contributed ideas, words, and definitions, but input has also been received from other sources. We express appreciation to the federal and state regulatory agencies that have provided resource materials, insights, and proofreading assistance. Without their assistance, this book would not have been possible.

PREFACE

Every person who must deal with banking terms, regulatory compliance reporting, and regulatory issues, has looked at some time for help in a dictionary. Unfortunately, the dictionaries published for general use do not fill the needs of bankers. This book is an attempt to fill some of the gaps. It is not an exhaustive list of every banking term, regulatory definition, regulatory word, and regulatory/banking phrase, but is a bringing together of the common terms, phrases, etc. for which people occasionally need precise definitions. Our focus is on the major issues, the major regulations, and the major acronyms. As the banking and regulatory environment changes, we will review the need to update this edition and include more words.

Note: Confer with legal counsel and review regulatory reference materials before reaching decisions rather than relying strictly on this document as a sole source for guidance. Materials such as this become dated and may not address current issues; the bulk, however, will still be valid in twenty years. Not many publications can carry such a life span.

CONTENTS

INTRODUCTION

There is minimal introduction required for a book of this type. Rather, the only introduction is to encourage you as a reader to take time to leaf through it and acquaint yourself with the reference materials. Note that some words have specific relationships with the regulation cited. Also, note that some words are defined differently by different regulations. To assist readers in dealing with such regulations and word definitions, we have included a glossary of important regulations with cross-references to key terms.

We are already utilizing this book in our daily activities. Its usefulness grows each week. We trust that it will serve you as well as it has served us.

ABOUT THE AUTHOR

REGULATORY COMPLIANCE ASSOCIATES, INC. (also known as REGCOM) was established to provide regulatory compliance products and services for financial institutions. Established in 1988, the firm has provided consulting assistance to accounting firms, trade associations, financial institutions, and other business firms supporting the financial industry. REGCOM has the expertise and resources to address a wide assortment of projects, such as assisting bank management develop, implement (including staff training), and subsequently test the use of manual or automated regulatory compliance reference materials and the related controls, or performing on-site compliance reviews.

President Jerry Miller was formerly with Peat Marwick Main & Co., where he served as practice leader for the Financial Institutions Regulatory Compliance Consulting practice. In this role, Mr. Miller and his associates advised management and directorates of financial institutions on understanding and complying with regulations.

Mr. Miller and his associates gained valuable experience while serving as field examiners and members of the Regional/District management team of federal banking regulatory agencies. The REGCOM staff has significant financial, regulatory, and problem bank assistance expertise, including participating in the development and implementation of Regional, District, and National regulatory policies and guidelines pertaining to various aspects of banking. Members of REGCOM's staff have written numerous articles on compliance and banking, and are frequent lecturers at financial institution conferences.

(Continued)

In summary, REGCOM's staff is composed of individuals with a wide range of financial institution and regulatory compliance experience. Members of the staff are assigned to projects according to subject matter expertise, providing REGCOM clients with the assurance that they are getting the "best" professionals to help them with their institution's problems or concerns.

For further information
please contact:

MR. JERRY MILLER, PRESIDENT
REGULATORY COMPLIANCE ASSOCIATES, INC.
P.O. Box 446
GENEVA, ILLINOIS 60134
(312) 232-7342

SECTION I

Regulatory Compliance Dictionary

A

Acceptance

A time draft (such as bill of exchange) drawn by one party and acknowledged by a second party. The drawee, known as the "acceptor," stamps or writes the word "accepted" on the face of the draft and above his or her signature the place and date of payment. Once the draft is accepted, it carries an unconditional obligation on the part of the acceptor to pay the drawer the amount of the draft on the date specified.

Accepted Access Device

REGULATION E, 12 CFR 205.2 (a) (2)

"An access device, as defined below, becomes an 'accepted access device' when the consumer to whom the access device was issued:

(i) requests and receives, or signs, or uses, or authorizes another to use, the access device for the purpose of transferring money between accounts or obtaining money, property, labor, or services;

(ii) requests validation of an access device issued on an unsolicited basis; or

(iii) receives an access device issued in renewal of, or in substitution for, an accepted access device, whether such access device is issued by the initial financial institution or a successor."

Access Device

REGULATION E, 12 CFR 205.2 (a) (1)

"A card, code, or other means of access to a consumer's account, or any combination thereof, that may by used by the consumer for the purpose of initiating electronic fund transfers."

Account

A listing of the financial transactions by date, which affect an individual phase of a business or an individual. All entries are expressed in debits and credits, and are evaluated in money, and reflect the current balance, if any.

REGULATION B, 12 CFR 202.2 (a)

"An extension of credit."

REGULATION E, 12 CFR 205.2 (b)

"A demand deposit (checking), savings, or other consumer asset account (other than an occasional or incidental credit balance in a credit plan) held either directly or indirectly by a financial institution and established primarily for personal, family, or household purposes."

REGULATION CC, 12 CFR 229.2 (a)

"A deposit as defined in 12 CFR 204.2(a)(1)(i) that is a transaction account as described in 12 CFR 204.2(e)."

As defined in these sections, *account* generally includes accounts at a bank from which the account holder is permitted to make transfers or withdrawals by negotiable or transferable instrument, payment order of withdrawal, telephone transfer, electronic payment, or other similar means for the purpose of making payments or transfers to third persons or others. *Account* also includes accounts at a bank from which the account holder may make third-party payments at an ATM, remote service unit, or other electronic device, including by debit card, but the term does not include savings deposits or accounts described in 12 CFR 204.2(d)(2) even though such accounts permit third-party transfers. An account may be in the form of ;

1. a demand deposit account,
2. a negotiable order of withdrawal account,
3. a share draft account,
4. an automatic transfer account, or
5. any other transaction account described in 12 CFR 204.2(e).

Account does not include an account where the account holder is a bank, where the account holder is an office of an institution described in paragraphs (e)(1) through (e)(6) of Section 2 of Regulation CC, or an office of a "foreign bank" as defined in Section 1(b) of the International Banking Act (12 USC 3101), which is located outside the U.S., or where the direct or indirect holder of the account is the Treasury of the U.S.

Accretion

The asset growth that occurs due to factors such as internal expansion, development, or acquisition. The term also refers to the accounting recognition of the value difference between the price of a security, that is, bond, purchased at one price and the par value of the bond.

Accretion Account

When a bond is purchased at a discount, the difference between the purchase price and the face value of the bond is reflected in this account.

Actually and Finally Collected Funds

PER REGULATION J, 12 CFR 210.2 (a)

Cash or any other form of payment that is, or has become, final and irrevocable.

Additional Paid-In Capital

Amounts received by a corporation in excess of the par or stated value of the capital stock at its initial issuance and from other subsequent transactions involving the institution's stock and stockholders.

Adjacent Cities, Towns, or Villages

REGULATION L, 12 CFR 212.2 (a)

"Cities, towns, or villages whose borders are within ten road miles of each other at their closest points. The property line of an office located in an unincorporated city, town, or village is regarded as the boundary line of that city, town, or village for the purposes of this definition."

Adjustable Rate Mortgage (ARM)

A type of mortgage loan that provides in its terms for periodic adjustment of the interest rate on the outstanding balance, which in turn causes a change in the balance, term to maturity, or payment level of the loan.

Administrator

An individual or a corporation appointed by a court to settle the estate of a person who has died without leaving a valid will.

Administrator (ERISA)

[As defined under ERISA] the person designated as administrator by the instrument under which the plan is operated. If the administrator is not so designated, *administrator* means the plan sponsor. If the administrator is not designated, and the plan sponsor cannot be identified, the administrator may be such person as is prescribed by regulation of the Secretary of Labor.

Adverse Action

REGULATION B, 12 CFR 202.2 (c)

(1)(i) "A refusal to grant credit in substantially the amount or on substantially the terms requested in an application unless the creditor makes a counteroffer (to grant credit in a different amount or on other terms) and the applicant uses or expressly accepts the credit offered;

(ii) A termination of an account or an unfavorable change in the terms of an account that does not affect all or a substantial portion of a class of the creditor's accounts; or

(iii) A refusal to increase the amount of credit available to an applicant who has made an application for an increase.

(2) The term does not include;

(i) a change in the terms of an account expressly agreed to by an applicant;

(ii) any action or forbearance relating to an account taken in connection with inactivity, default, or delinquency as to that account;

(iii) a refusal or failure to authorize an account transaction at a point of sale or loan, except when the refusal is a termination or an unfavorable change in the terms of an account that does not affect all or a substantial portion of a class of the creditor's accounts, or when the refusal is a denial of an application for an increase in the amount of credit available under the account;

(iv) a refusal to extend credit because applicable law prohibits the creditor from extending the credit requested; or

(v) a refusal to extend credit because the creditor does not offer the type of credit or credit plan requested.

(3) An action that falls within the definition of both paragraphs (1) and (2) is governed by paragraph (2)."

Advertisement

REGULATION M, 12 CFR 213.2 (a) (2)

"Any commercial message in any newspaper, magazine, leaflet, flyer, or catalog, on radio, television, or public address system, in direct mail literature or other printed material on any interior or exterior sign or display, in any window display, in any point-of-transaction literature or price tag which is delivered or made available to a lessee or prospective lessee in any manner whatsoever."

REGULATION Z, 12 CFR 226.2 (a) (2)

"A commercial message in any medium that promotes, directly or indirectly, a credit transaction."

Advised Letter of Credit

An export letter of credit issued by a bank that requests another bank to advise the beneficiary that the credit has been opened in its favor. This occurs when the issuing bank does not have an office in the country of the beneficiary and uses the facilities of a correspondent bank. An advised credit creates no liability on the part of the advising bank.

Advised Line of Credit

Customer notification of agreement between bank and customer indicating the bank's agreement to lend the customer funds up to a certain amount, subject to possibly certain requirements or guidelines that may be stated in the notification. The customer can draw against the preapproved line and make payments at a future date.

Affiliate

FEDERAL RESERVE ACT SECTION 23A (b) (1)

With respect to a bank that is a member of the Federal Reserve System:

(A) "Any company that controls the member bank and any other company that is controlled by the company that controls the member bank;

(B) A bank subsidiary of the member bank;

(C) Any company:

(i) that is controlled directly or indirectly, by a trust or otherwise, by or for the benefit of shareholders who beneficially or otherwise control, directly or indirectly, by trust or otherwise, the member bank or any company that controls the member bank; or

(ii) in which a majority of its directors or trustees constitute a majority of the persons holding any such office with the member bank or any company that controls the member bank;

(D)(i) any company, including a real estate investment trust, that is sponsored and advised on a contractual basis by the member bank or any subsidiary or affiliate of the member bank; or

(ii) any investment company with respect to which a member bank or any affiliate thereof is an investment advisor as defined in Section 2(a)(20) of the Investment Company Act of 1940; and

(E) any company that the Board determines by regulation or order to have a relationship with the member bank or any subsidiary or affiliate of the member bank, such that covered transactions by the member bank or its subsidiary with that company may be affected by the relationship to the detriment of the member bank or its subsidiary."

The following shall **not** be considered to be an affiliate:

(A) "Any company, other than a bank, that is a subsidiary of a member bank, unless a determination is made under item (E) above not to exclude such subsidiary company from the definition of affiliate;

(B) Any company engaged solely in holding the premises of the member bank;

(C) Any company engaged solely in conducting a safe deposit business;

(D) Any company engaged solely in holding obligations of the United States or its agencies or obligations fully guaranteed by the United States or its agencies as to principal and interest; and

(E) Any company where control results from the exercise of rights arising out of a bona fide debt previously contracted, but only for the period of time specifically authorized under applicable State or Federal law or regulation or, in the absence of such law or regulation, for a period of two years from the date of the exercise of such rights or the effective date of this Act, whichever date is later, subject, upon application, to authorization by the Board for good cause shown of extensions of time for not more than one year at a time, but such extensions in the aggregate shall not exceed three years."

PER REGULATION D, 12 CFR 204.2 (q)

Any corporation, association, or other organization;

1. of which a depository institution, directly or indirectly,

owns or controls either a majority of the voting shares or more than 50 percent of the numbers of shares voted for the election of its directors, trustees, or other persons exercising similar functions at the preceding election, or controls in any manner the election of a majority of its directors, trustees, or other persons exercising similar functions;

2. of which control is held, directly or indirectly, through stock ownership or in any other manner, by the shareholders of a depository institution or more than 50 percent of the number of shares voted for the election of directors of such depository institution at the preceding election, or by trustees for the benefit of the shareholders of any such depository institution;

3. of which a majority of its directors, trustees, or other persons exercising similar functions are directors of any one depository institution; or

4. which owns or controls, directly or indirectly, either a majority of the shares of capital stock of a depository institution or more than 50 percent of the number of shares voted for the election of directors, trustees, or other persons exercising similar functions of a depository institution at the preceding election, or controls in any manner the election of a majority of the directors, trustees, or other persons exercising similar functions of a depository institution, or for the benefit of whose shareholders or members all or substantially all the capital stock of a depository institution is held by trustees.

REGULATION K, 12 CFR 211.2(a)

(1) "Any entity of which an organization is a direct or indirect subsidiary; or

(2) Any direct or indirect subsidiary of the organization or such entity."

REGULATION L, 12 CFR 212.2 (b)

"Affiliate has the meaning given in Section 202 of the Interlocks Act; for purposes of Section 202, an individual's shares include shares of members of his or her immediate family. For the purpose of Section 202(3)(b) of the Interlocks Act, an affiliate relationship based on common ownership does not exist if the appropriate federal supervisory agency or agencies determine, after giving the affected persons the opportunity to respond, that the asserted affiliation appears to have been established in order to avoid the prohibitions of the Interlocks Act and does not represent a true commonality of interest between the depository organizations. In making this determination, the agencies will consider, among other things, whether a person, including members of his or her immediate family, whose shares are necessary to constitute the group owns a nominal percentage of the shares of one of the organizations and the percentage is substantially disproportionate with that person's ownership of shares in the other organization. 'Immediate family' includes spouse, mother, father, child, grandchild, sister, brother, or any of their spouses, whether or not any of their shares are held in trust."

REGULATION U, 12 CFR 221.2 (a)

(1) "Any bank holding company of which a bank is a subsidiary within the meaning of the Bank Holding Company Act of 1956, as amended (12 USC 1841[d]);

(2) Any other subsidiary of such bank holding company; and

(3) Any other corporation, business trust, association, or other similar organization that is an affiliate as defined in Section 2(b) of the Banking Act of 1933 (12 USC 221a[c])."

Affiliated Person

Officer, director, or controlling person of an institution, including their immediate family members. Also refers to any corporation or organization in which the officer, director, controlling person, or his or her immediate family members have a specific ownership position. *See also* AFFILIATE.

Age

REGULATION B, 12 CFR 202.2 (d)

Refers to age of natural persons and means the number of fully elapsed years from the date of an applicant's birth.

Agent Bank

The bank that leads and documents a syndicated loan, selling participations to others.

Aggregate Amount of Covered Transactions

FEDERAL RESERVE ACT, SECTION 23A (b) (8); (12 USC 371 [b] [8])

"The amount of the covered transactions about to be engaged in, added to the current amount of all outstanding covered transactions." *See* COVERED TRANSACTIONS.

Agreement

Formal administrative action. Written agreement between a regulatory agency and the board of directors of a bank, whereby the board of directors consents to do certain things in compliance with laws and regulations to restore the bank to a safe and sound condition. Noncompliance with an agreement can lead to an order to cease and desist.

Agreement Corporation

A state-chartered corporation that has agreed to operate as if it were organized under Section 25 of the Federal Reserve Act and has agreed to be subject to Federal Reserve Regulation K. Agreement corporations are restricted, in general, to international banking operations. Banks must apply to the Federal Reserve for permission to acquire stock in an agreement corporation.

Agricultural Purpose

REGULATION M, 12 CFR 213.2 (a) (3)

"A purpose related to the production, harvest, exhibition, marketing, transportation, processing, or manufacture of agricultural products by a natural person who cultivates, plants, propagates, or nurtures those agricultural products, including, but not limited to, the acquisition of personal property and services used primarily in farming. 'Agricultural products' includes agricultural, horticultural, viticultural, and dairy products, livestock, wildlife, poultry, bees, forest products, fish and shellfish, and any products thereof, including processed and manufactured products, and any and all products raised or produced on farms and any processed or manufactured products thereof."

Allowance for Loan and Lease Losses

A valuation allowance established and replenished by charges against operating income to provide a balance for absorbing possible losses in an institution's loan portfolio. Capital calculation ratios and adequacy assessments include the allowance for loan and lease losses.

American Banker's Association (ABA)

An association formed in 1875 with the purpose of "promoting the general welfare and usefulness of banks and financial institutions."

Amortization

Paying off an interest-bearing liability by gradual reduction through a series of installments, as opposed to one lump-sum payment. A technique for gradually extinguishing a liability, deferred charge, or capital expenditure. Includes such practices as depreciation, depletion, write-off of intangibles, prepaid expenses, and deferred charges (that is, mortgages are amortized by periodically retiring part of the face amount). The liquidation of a debt on an installment basis.

Annual Percentage Rate (APR)

The cost of credit on a yearly basis expressed as a percentage.

Applicant

PER REGULATION B, 12 CFR 202.2 (e)

A person who requests or has received an extension of credit from a creditor, and includes any person who is or may become contractually liable regarding an extension of credit. For purposes of Regulation B, Section 202.7(d) the term includes guarantors, sureties, endorsers, and similar parties.

Application

REGULATION B, 12 CFR 202.2 (f)

"An oral or written request for an extension of credit that is made in accordance with procedures established by a creditor for the type of credit requested. The term does not include the use of an account or line of credit to obtain an amount of credit that is within a previously established credit limit. A completed application means an application in connection with which a creditor has received all the information that the creditor regularly obtains and considers in evaluating applications for the amount and type of credit requested (including, but not limited to, credit reports, any additional information requested from the applicant, and any approvals or reports by governmental agencies or other persons that are necessary to guarantee, insure, or provide security for the credit or collateral). The creditor shall exercise reasonable diligence in obtaining such information."

Appreciation

In general, an increase in value of property. For example, a rise in the value of a currency relative to the value of another currency.

Arbitrage

Simultaneous buying and selling of foreign currencies or of securities and commodities to realize profits from discrepancies between currencies, securities, or goods in separate markets. It may also be the exchange rates prevailing at the same time in different markets or between forward margins for different maturities.

Asset Yield

Operating interest income divided by total assets.

Asset/Liability Structure

Relationship between risk and return, as created and existing by the combination and growth of certain assets and liabilities. Return on the asset/liability structure is measured by net interest margin, return on assets, return on equity, equity growth. Inherent risks include liquidity risk, credit risk, interest rate risk, gap and maturity risk, capital risk, and regulatory risk.

Associated Company

Consolidated Reports of Condition and Income Instructions: A corporation in which the bank, directly or indirectly, owns 20 to 50 percent of the outstanding voting stock and over which the bank exercises significant influence. This 20 to 50 percent ownership is presumed to carry "significant" influence unless the bank can demonstrate the contrary to the satisfaction of the appropriate federal supervisory authority.

Audit Date

The "as of" date for the audit review. For example, the "as of" date for a financial audit would be the business date for which all financial accounts, transactions, and information would be audited.

Audit Plan

Comprehensive, overall detailed guidance for the organization that begins with the assessment of audit risks for each functional area, and sections of the functional areas. The written audit plan should clearly set out audit objectives and planned audit coverage.

Audit Program

A written guide for the orderly performance and completion of the audit to be performed, including listing of procedures to be completed during the audit.

Audit Trail

A means of identifying the actions taken in processing input data or in preparing an output such that data on a source document can be traced forward to an output (a report for example), and an output can be traced back to the source items from which it is derived.

Automated Clearinghouse (ACH)

A computer-based clearing and settlement operation, often operated by a Federal Reserve Bank, established for the exchange of electronic transactions among participating depository institutions. Such electronic transactions can be substituted for paper checks used to make recurring payments such as payroll or preauthorized insurance premiums. The U.S. Treasury uses an ACH extensively to pay certain obligations of the government.

REGULATION CC, 12 CFR 229.2 (b)

A facility that processes debit and credit transfers under rules established by a Federal Reserve Bank operating circular on automated clearinghouse items or under rules of an automated clearinghouse association.

Automated Teller Machines (ATM)

Computer-controlled terminals located on the premises of financial institutions or elsewhere, through which customers may make deposits, withdrawals, or other transactions as they would through a bank teller. Other terms sometimes used to describe such terminals are customer-bank communications terminal (CBCT) and remote service unit (RSU). Groups of banks sometimes share ATM networks located throughout a region of the country, which may include portions of several states.

REGULATION CC, 12 CFR 229.2 (c)

An electronic device at which a natural person may make deposits to an account by cash or check and perform other account transactions.

Automated Transfer Service (ATS) Account

A depositor's savings account from which funds may be transferred automatically to the same depositor's checking account to cover a check written or to maintain a minimum balance.

Available for Withdrawal

REGULATION CC, 12 CFR 229.2 (d)

"With respect to funds deposited means available for all uses generally permitted to the customer for actually and finally collected funds under the bank's account agreement or policies, such as for payment of checks drawn on the account, certification of checks drawn on the account, electronic payments, withdrawals by cash, and transfers between accounts."

B

Backup

Pertaining to equipment or procedures that are available for use in the event of failure or overloading of normally used equipment or procedures.

Bait Money

Currency handed out during a robbery; bills are identified in advance by recording serial numbers. In the event of a robbery, the numbers are given to federal enforcement agents in assisting them to recover the stolen money. Other types of Bait Money have also been developed; for example, spraying a color of nonwashable dye or releasing some other substance that will mark all the stolen money. These special marking effects usually occur several minutes after the robber leaves the premises.

Balloon Payment

A scaled method of bond interest or mortgage payment that allows for a final payment substantially higher than previous payments.

Bank

REGULATION J, 12 CFR 210.2 (b)

"A depository institution as defined in Section 19 of the Federal Reserve Act (12 USC 461[b])."

REGULATION U, 12 CFR 221.2 (b)

(1) "'Bank' has the meaning given to it in Section 3(a)(6) of the Securities Exchange Act (15 USC 78c[a][6]) and includes

(i) any subsidiary of a bank;

(ii) any corporation organized under Section 25(a) of the Federal Reserve Act (12 USC 611); and

(iii) any agency or branch of a foreign bank located within the United States.

(2) 'Bank' does not include

(i) any savings and loan association

(ii) any credit union

(ii) any lending institution that is an instrumentality or agency of the United States, or

(iv) any member of a national securities exchange."

REGULATION CC, 12 CFR 229.2 (e)

(1) "An 'insured bank' as defined in Section 3 of the Federal Deposit Insurance Act (12 USC 1813) or a bank that is eligible to apply to become an insured bank under section 5 of that act (12 USC 1815);

(2) A 'mutual savings bank' as defined in Section 3 of the Federal Deposit Insurance Act (12 USC 1813);

(3) A 'savings bank' as defined in Section 3 of the Federal Deposit Insurance Act (12 USC 1813);

(4) An 'insured credit union' as defined in Section 101 of the Federal Credit Union Act (12 USC 1752) or a credit union that is eligible to make application to become an insured credit union under Section 201 of that act (12 USC 1781);

(5) A 'member' as defined in Section 2 of the Federal Home Loan Bank Act (12 USC 1422);

(6) An 'insured institution' as defined in Section 401 of the National Housing Act (12 USC 1724) or an institution that is eligible to make application to become an insured institution under Section 403 of that act (12 USC 1726); or

(7) An 'agency' or 'branch' of a 'foreign bank'as defined in Section 1(b) of the International Banking Act (12 USC 3101).

For purposes of subpart C of Regulation CC and, in connection therewith, subpart A, the term 'bank' also includes any person engaged in the business of banking, including a Federal Reserve Bank, a Federal Home Loan Bank, and a state or unit of general local government to the extent that the state or unit of general local government acts as a paying bank. Unless otherwise specified, the term 'bank' includes all of a bank's offices in the United States, but not offices located outside the United States."

Bank Administration Institute (BAI)

Bank Administration Institute, formerly known as the National Association of Bank Auditors and Comptrollers, was founded in 1924. The purpose of this organization is to formulate and encourage programs, publications, and other resourcing efforts that support and promote quality auditing and operating procedures at all banks.

Bank Draft

REGULATION J, 12 CFR 210.2 (c)

"A check drawn by one bank on another bank."

Bank for International Settlements (BIS)

The BIS, located in Basel, Switzerland, was established in 1930 to administer the post–World War I reparations agreements. Since the 1960s, the BIS has evolved into an important international monetary institution and has provided a forum in which central bankers meet and consult on a monthly basis. As an independent financial organization, the BIS performs a variety of banking, trustee, and agent functions, primarily with central banks. At present the BIS has 29 members, 28 of which are central banks. The Federal Reserve is represented at BIS meetings, but it is not a member. The BIS is the only international financial institution in which most Eastern European countries are members. The Soviet Union, East Germany, and Albania, however, are not members.

Bank Holding Company

A company that owns or controls one or more banks. The Federal Reserve Board of Governors has responsibility for regulating and supervising bank holding companies, such as approving acquisitions and mergers and inspecting the operations of such companies. This authority applies even though a bank owned by a holding company may be under the primary supervision of the Comptroller of the Currency, the FDIC, or respective state banking divisions.

Bank Secrecy Act (BSA)

The Bank Secrecy Act was enacted in October 1970. It has two primary purposes: curtail the laundering of money in the United States, and detect any attempts to launder money through cash transactions with financial institutions through traceable procedures and forms. *See* 31 USC 5311 and 31 CFR 103.

Banker's Acceptance (BA)

Banker's acceptances are negotiable time drafts or bills of exchange that have been accepted by a bank, which, by accepting, assumes the obligation to pay the holder of the draft the face amount of the instrument on the maturity date specified. They are used primarily to finance the export, import, shipment, or storage of goods. *See also* TIME DRAFT and BILLS OF EXCHANGE.

Banker's Bill

Negotiable draft without supporting papers drawn by one bank upon its credit balance at a foreign bank.

Banking Day

REGULATION J, 12 CFR 210.2 (d)

"A day during which a bank is open to the public for carrying on substantially all its banking functions."

REGULATION CC, 12 CFR 229.2 (f)

"That part of any business day on which an office of a bank is open to the public for carrying on substantially all of its banking functions."

Banking Hours

REGULATION P, 12 CFR 216.1 (b)

"The time during which a banking office is open for the normal transaction of business with the banking public."

Banking Office

REGULATION P, 12 CFR 215.1 (c)

"The main office of any state member bank and any branch thereof."

Basis Risk

The risk that the yield and price correlation between a hedged item and a hedging vehicle could change.

Beneficial Interest

The interest of a beneficiary, as opposed to the interest of a trustee who holds legal title; the equitable interest in property held in trust, which the beneficiary may enforce against the trustee according to the terms of the trust.

Beneficiary

(1) The person for whose benefit a trust is created.

(2) The person to whom the amount of an insurance policy or annuity is payable.

(3) The person or company in whose favor a letter of credit is opened or a draft is drawn.

Bill of Exchange

An unconditional order written from one person (the drawer) to another person (the drawee) directing the latter to pay a certain sum of money at a fixed or future determinable date to the order of a third party. The terms *bill of exchange* and *draft* are generally used interchangeably.

Billing Cycle

REGULATION Z, 12 CFR 226.2 (a) (4)

"Means the interval between the days or dates of regular periodic statements. These intervals shall be equal in length and no longer than a quarter of a year. An interval will be considered equal if the number of days in the cycle does not vary more than four days from the regular day or date of the periodic statement."

Blue List (of Current Municipal Offerings)

A daily service published by Standard and Poor's Corporation, listing municipal bonds offered publicly by dealers. (This accounts for approximately 40 percent of the municipals available in the national market.)

Blue Sky Laws

State laws concerning the registration and issuance of securities; these may be different from federal laws and regulations, and generally must be obeyed if a security is to be sold in that state.

Borrowing Authorization

Agreement or resolution that authorizes certain individuals to borrow funds on behalf of a corporation or partnership.

Branch

REGULATION P, 12 CFR 216.1 (d)

"Any branch bank, branch office, branch agency, additional office, or any branch place of business located in any state of the United States, or in any territory of the United States, Puerto Rico, Guam, or the Virgin Islands at which deposits are received or checks paid or money lent."

Branch Office (BO)

REGULATION C, 12 CFR 203.2 (b)

(1)(i) "Any office of a financial institution that is approved as a branch by a federal or state supervisory agency; or

(ii) for a financial institution that is not required to obtain approval for a branch office, any office of the institution that takes applications from the public for home-purchase or home-improvement loans.

(2) The term excludes free-standing automated teller machines and other electronic terminals."

Bribery

Act of giving, providing, or offering something of value, such as money or a favor, to someone in a position of trust to induce that person to do something or act dishonestly or to influence performance of an official duty.

Brokered Deposits

Brokered deposits represent deposits that the reporting bank receives from brokers or dealers for the account of others either directly or ultimately. Brokered deposits include both those in which the entire beneficial interest in a given deposit instrument issued by the bank is held by a single depositor and those in which the broker sells participations in a given bank instrument to one or more investors.

Brokered Retail Deposits

Brokered deposits that are issued in denominations of $100,000 or less or that are issued in denominations greater than $100,000 and participated out by the broker in shares of $100,000 or less. *See* **Brokered Deposits.**

Broker's Security Draft

A draft with securities or title to securities attached, which is drawn to obtain payment for the securities. This draft is sent to a bank for collection with instructions to release the securities only on payment of the draft.

Business Day

REGULATION E, 12 CFR 205.2 (d)

"Any day on which the offices of the consumer's financial institution are open to the public for carrying on substantially all business functions."

REGULATION Z, 12 CFR 226.2 (a) (6)

"A day on which a creditor's offices are open to the public for carrying on substantially all of its business functions. However, for purposes of rescission under Section 226.15 and 226.23 of Regulation Z, the term means all calendar days except Sundays and the legal public holidays specified in 5 USC 6103(a), such as New Year's Day, Washington's Birthday, Memorial Day, Independence Day, Labor Day, Columbus Day, Veterans Day, Thanksgiving Day, and Christmas Day."

REGULATION CC, 12 CFR 229.2 (g)

"A calendar day other than a Saturday or a Sunday, January 1, the third Monday in January, the third Monday in February, the last Monday in May, July 4, the first Monday in September, the second Monday in October, November 11, the fourth Thursday in November, or December 25. If January 1, July 4, November 11, or December 25 fall on a Sunday, the next Monday is not a business day."

C

Call Option

An optional forward purchase contract representing an option to buy an asset within a given period of time at a specific price fixed in a contract. It obligates the seller of the contract to sell some financial instrument at the option of the buyer of the contract.

Call Report

A generic term for what every national bank, state member bank, and insured state nonmember bank is required to file as consolidated Reports of Condition and Income, normally as of the last calendar day of each calendar quarter; that is, the report date. Banks are required to prepare and file the Reports of Condition and Income in accordance with instructions prepared by the Federal Financial Institutions Examination Council and to submit them to the Federal Deposit Insurance Corporation, for national banks and state nonmember banks, and to the appropriate Federal Reserve Bank for state member banks. For purposes of this dictionary, these reports are referred to as "Call Reports."

Capital

In its most generic terminology, *capital* refers to a bank or bank holding company's funds resulting from the sale of stock, bonds, or notes issued by the bank or bank holding company, and also its retained earnings.

REGULATION H, 12 CFR 208.1 (f)

"Common stock, preferred stock, and legally issued capital notes and debentures purchased by the Reconstruction Finance Corporation, which may be considered capital and capital stock for purposes of membership in the Federal Reserve System under the provisions of Section 9 of the Federal Reserve Act."

For purposes of other regulatory agencies, *capital* includes the amount of common stock outstanding and unimpaired, plus the amount of preferred stock outstanding and unimpaired.

Capital and Surplus

REGULATION K, 12 CFR 211.2 (b)

"Paid-in and unimpaired capital and surplus, which includes undivided profits but does not include the proceeds of capital notes or debentures."

Capital Plan

A written, formal strategy that is developed, adopted, and implemented by an institution's board of directors to meet, exceed, or at least maintain certain capital goals, usually over a three-to-five year period.

Capital Stock

The designated amount of stock a banking organization may sell as authorized by the governing regulatory supervisory authority approved in the granting of the corporate charter. If the stock has a stated value per share, the value is known as par value. Otherwise, the stock is nonpar stock.

For regulatory purposes, *capital stock* is frequently used as a synonymous term for capital.

Card Issuer

REGULATION Z, 12 CFR 226.2 (a) (7)

"A person or company that issues a credit card or that person's agent with respect to the card."

Cardholder

REGULATION Z, 12 CFR 226.2 (a) (8)

"A natural person to whom a credit card is issued for consumer credit purposes, or a natural person who has agreed with the card issuer to pay consumer credit obligations arising from the issuance of a credit card to another natural person. For purposes of Section 226.12(a) and (b), the term includes any person to whom a credit card is issued for any purpose, including business, commercial, or agricultural use, or a person who has agreed with the card issuer to pay obligations arising from the issuance of such a credit card to another person."

Carrying Credit

REGULATION U, 12 CFR 221.2 (c)

"Credit that enables a customer to maintain, reduce, or retire indebtedness originally incurred to purchase a security that is currently a margin stock."

Cash

REGULATION CC, 12 CFR 229.2 (h)

"United States coins and currency."

Cash Dividends

Payments of cash to stockholders in proportion to the number of shares they own.Cash dividends are normally declared by an institution's board of directors on a quarterly, semiannual or annual basis, based upon that period's earnings.

Cash Flow

Calculated by adding amounts recognized for depreciation, depletion, amortization, and extraordinary charges to reserves, to the net income figure. This figure gives a better indication of the ability of a company to service debt and, secondarily, to pay dividends than does "net income."

Cash Item

Any item immediately convertible into cash.

REGULATION J, 12 CFR 210.2 (e)

(1) "A check other than one classified as a noncash item under Section 2 of Regulation J; or

(2) any other item payable on demand and collectible at par that the Reserve Bank of the District in which the item is payable is willing to accept as a cash item. 'Cash item' does not include a returned check."

Cash Item in Process of Collection

REGULATION D, 12 CFR 204.2 (i)

(1)(i) "Checks in the process of collection, drawn on a bank or other depository institution that are payable immediately upon presentation in the United States, including checks forwarded to a Federal Reserve Bank in process of collection and checks on hand that will be presented for payment or forwarded for collection on the following business day;

(ii) government checks drawn on the Treasury of the United States that are in the process of collection; and

(iii) such other items in the process of collection that are payable immediately upon presentation in the United States and that are customarily cleared or collected by depository institutions as cash items, including;

(A) drafts payable through another depository institution;

(B) redeemed bonds and coupons;

(C) food coupons and certificates;

(D) postal and other money orders, and traveler's checks;

(E) amounts credited to deposit accounts in connection with automated payment arrangements where such credits are made one business day prior to the scheduled payment date to insure that funds are available on the payment date;

(F) commodity or bill of lading drafts payable immediately upon presentation in the United States;

(G) returned items and unposted debits; and

(H) broker security drafts.

(2) 'Cash item in process of collection' does not include items handled as noncash collections and credit card sales slips and drafts."

Cash Letter of Credit

A letter addressed from one bank to one of its correspondents making available to the party named in the letter a fixed sum of money up to a future specific date. The sum indicated in the letter is equal to an amount deposited in the issuing bank by the party before the letter is issued.

Cash Price

REGULATION Z, 12 CFR 226.2 (a) (9)

"The price at which a creditor, in the ordinary course of business, offers to sell for cash the property or service that is the subject of the transaction. At the creditor's option, the term may include the price of accessories, service related to the sale, service contracts, and taxes and fees for license, title, and registration. The term does not include any finance charge."

Cashier's Check

A bank's own check drawn upon itself.

REGULATION CC, 12 CFR 229.2 (i)

"A check that is

(1) Drawn on a bank;

(2) Signed by an officer or employee of the bank on behalf of the bank as drawer;

(3) A direct obligation of the bank; and

(4) Provided to a customer of the bank or acquired from the bank for remittance purposes."

Cease and Desist Order

A formal administrative order issued after notice and opportunity for hearing, requiring a depository institution, a holding company, or a depository institution official to terminate unlawful, unsafe, or unsound banking practices. Cease-and-desist orders are issued by the appropriate federal regulatory agencies under the Financial Institutions Supervisory Act, and noncompliance can be enforced directly by the courts. Violations of cease-and-desist orders can result in civil money penalties.

Certificate of Deposit (CD)

A form of time deposit at a bank or savings institution; a time deposit that cannot be withdrawn before a specified maturity date without being subject to an interest penalty for early withdrawal. Small-denomination CDs are often purchased by individuals. Large CDs of $100,000 or more are often in negotiable form, meaning they can be sold or transferred among holders before maturity.

Certified Check

PER REGULATION CC, 12 CFR 229.2 (j)

"A check with respect to which the drawee bank certifies by signature on the check of an officer or other authorized employee of the bank that

(1)(i) The signature of the drawer on the check is genuine; and

(ii) The bank has set aside funds that

(A) Are equal to the amount of the check, and

(B) Will be used to pay the check;

(2) The bank will pay the check upon presentment."

Charge Card

REGULATION Z, 12 CFR 226.2 (a) (15)

"A credit card on an account for which no periodic rate is used to compute a finance charge."

Check

REGULATION CC, 12 CFR 229.2 (k)

(1) "A negotiable demand draft drawn on or payable through or at an office of a bank;

(2) A negotiable demand draft drawn on a Federal Reserve Bank or a Federal Home Loan Bank;

(3) A negotiable demand draft drawn on the Treasury of the United States;

(4) A demand draft drawn on a state government or unit of general local government that is not payable through or at a bank;

(5) A United States Postal Service money order; or

(6) A traveler's check drawn on or payable through or at a bank. The term 'check' does not include a noncash item or an item payable in a medium other than United States money. A draft may be a check even though it is described on its face by another term, such as 'money order.' For purposes of Subpart C of Regulation CC, and in connection therewith, Subpart A of Regulation CC, the term 'check' also includes a demand draft of the type described above that is nonnegotiable."

REGULATION J, 12 CFR 210.2 (f)

"A draft, as defined in the Uniform Commercial Code, that is drawn on a bank and payable on demand. 'Check as defined in 12 CFR 229.2(k)' means an item defined as a check in 12 CFR 229.2(k) for purposes of Subpart C of Part 229."

Check Clearing

The movement of checks from the banks or other depository institutions where they are deposited back to those on which they are drawn and funds movement in the opposite direction. This process results in credits to accounts at the institutions of deposit and corresponding debits to the accounts at the paying institutions. The Federal Reserve participates in check clearing through its nationwide facilities, though many checks are cleared by private-sector arrangements.

Check Clearinghouse Association

REGULATION CC, 12 CFR 229.2 (l)

"Any arrangement by which three or more participants exchange checks on a local basis, including an entire metropolitan area. The term 'check clearinghouse association' may include arrangements using the premises of a Federal Reserve Bank, but it does not include the handling of checks for forward collection or return by a Federal Reserve Bank."

Check Credit

A form of unsecured, open-end consumer credit. Borrower finances purchase by writing a check, not unlike using a credit card.

Check Overdraft Protection

Form of unsecured, open-end consumer credit. A prearranged authorized line is created providing coverage and, thereby, advances in instances when the checking account is overdrawn.

Check Processing Region

PER REGULATION CC, 12 CFR 229.2 (m)

"The geographical area served by an office of a Federal Reserve Bank for purposes of its check-processing activities."

Chinese Wall

Policies and procedures established to ensure compliance with appropriate securities laws in connection with any decision or recommendation to purchase or sell any security. Such policies and procedures should ensure that trust departments do not utilize material inside information in connection with any decision or recommendation to purchase or sell any security.

Civil Money Penalties

Monetary penalties which may be assessed by supervisory agencies against financial institutions and their officers, directors, employees, and agents who have violated specified federal banking laws or regulations. Civil money penalties can also be assessed for violations of cease-and-desist orders or other requirements. Penalties are assessed on a per day basis and a notice of penalty and a notice of penalty is issued to the person or institution charged. Subsequent rules exist regarding subsequent hearings and related actions.

Clean Bill of Lading

A bill of lading in which the described merchandise has been received in "apparent good order and condition" and without qualification.

Clean Draft

A sight or time draft to which no other documents such as shipping documents, bills of lading, or insurance certificates are attached. This is to be distinguished from a documentary draft. *See* DOCUMENTARY DRAFT.

Clearing Institution

REGULATION J, 12 CFR 210.2 (l) (2)

"(i) An institution that is not a depository institution, but maintains with a Reserve Bank the balance referred to in the first paragraph of Section 13 of the Federal Reserve Act (12 USC 342); or

(ii) a corporation that maintains an account with a Reserve Bank in conformity withSection 211.4 of Regulation K."

Closed-end Credit

A credit agreement that specifies the total amount of credit, the number of payments, and the due date of payments.

REGULATION Z, 12 CFR 226.2 (a) (10)

"Consumer credit other than 'open-end credit'." *See* OPEN-END CREDIT.

Collateralized Mortgage Obligation (CMO)

Mortgage-backed security, separating mortgage pools into

various terms, usually short term (5-year), medium term (10- to 15-year) and long term (20-year). Each class or designation of security has a fixed rate of return at regular intervals.

Commercial Letter of Credit

A letter of credit issued specifically to facilitate trade or commerce. Under the terms of a commercial letter of credit, as a general rule, drafts will be drawn when the underlying transaction is consummated as intended.

Commercial Loan

Extension of credit for activities of business other than the acquisition and holding of real estate.

Commercial Paper

Commercial paper consists of short-term negotiable promissory notes issued in the United States by commercial businesses, including finance companies and banks. Commercial paper usually matures in 270 days or less and is not collateralized. Commercial paper may be backed by a standby letter of credit from a bank, as in the case of documented discounted notes.

Commodity or Bill-of-Lading Draft

A commodity or bill-of-lading draft is a draft that is issued in connection with the shipment of goods. If the commodity or bill-of-lading draft becomes payable only when the shipment of goods against which it is payable arrives, it is an arrival draft.

Arrival drafts are usually forwarded by the shipper to the collecting depository institution with instructions to release the shipping documents (for example, bill of lading) conveying title to the goods only upon payment of the draft. Payment, however, cannot be demanded until the goods have arrived at the drawee's destination. Arrival drafts provide a means of insuring payment of shipped goods at the time that the goods are released.

Common Stock

Securities that represent the proportionate amount of corporate ownership in a bank or bank holding company, which gives the holder an unlimited proportionate interest in the bank or bank holding company's assets and earnings after claims of creditors and holders of preferred stock have been fulfilled.

Community

REGULATION L, 12 CFR 212.2 (c)

"City, town, or village, or contiguous or adjacent cities, towns, or villages."

Community Reinvestment Act (CRA)

The Community Reinvestment Act (CRA) was enacted in 1977 with the purpose of requiring each federal financial supervisory agency to use its authority when conducting examinations to encourage the financial institutions it supervises to help meet the credit needs of its community, including low- and moderate-income neighborhoods, consistent with the financial institution's safe and sound operation. Each agency has implemented the Act through its own regulation. *See* Regulation BB.

Company

REGULATION O, 12 CFR 215.2 (a)

"Any corporation, partnership, trust (business or otherwise), association, joint venture, pool syndicate, sole proprietorship, unincorporated organization, or any other form of business entity not specifically listed herein. However, the term does not include

(1) an insured bank (as defined in 12 USC 1813[h]) or

(2) a corporation the majority of the shares of which are owned by the United States or by any state."

PER FEDERAL RESERVE ACT SECTION 23 A (b) (6)

A corporation, partnership, business trust, association, or

similar organization and, unless specifically excluded, the term *company* includes a "member bank" and a "bank."

Comptroller of the Currency

The Comptroller of the Currency (agency also known as the OCC) is an officer of the Treasury Department; the Office of the Comptroller of the Currency is responsible for chartering national banks and has primary supervisory authority over them. All national banks are required to be members of the Federal Reserve System and are insured by the Federal Deposit Insurance Corporation.

Concentration of Credit

A group of assets, direct, indirect, or contingent, which amount to a significant risk, and, thereby, a large exposure to the financial institution. Concentrations may include but are not limited to all loans of all types including overdrafts; cash items; suspense items; securities purchased or held under resale agreement; federal funds sold and other interbank deposits or loans; loan commitments, leases, and acceptances; letters of credit; placements; loans subject to repurchase agreements; and other types of direct, indirect, or contingent obligations. Concentrations are identified based on the dependency on one entity, one industry, one person, or one affiliated group to provide payment.

Concentrations are dependent on a key issue or element, such as loans to one borrower; loans to one group; loans to one industry group; loans to major employers, their employees, and major suppliers; loans dependent on common repayment source; loans in a specific geographic area; and participation loans purchased from a single source. Generally, 25 percent of primary capital is considered the determinant for a concentration of credit.

Confirmed Letter of Credit

A letter of credit issued by a bank that bears the confirmation of the seller's (exporter's) bank. The "confirming" bank undertakes to honor the draft drawn in accordance with the terms of the letter of credit. Thus, the beneficiary has the unconditional assurance that, if the issuing bank refused to honor the draft against the credit, the confirming bank will pay (or accept) it. In many instances, the seller (exporter) will ask that the letter of credit be confirmed by another bank since the seller is not familiar with the foreign issuing bank and as a precaution against unfavorable exchange regulations, foreign currency shortages, political upheavals, and similar situations that may arise in the foreign country.

Conflict of Interest

Situation wherein the safety and the soundness of an institution or the opportunity of that institution are in conflict with the personal interests of its director(s), officer(s), and other persons with influence over the management supervision of the institution.

Consolidation

The combining of the assets, liabilities, and capital accounts of two banks into a new bank. Both banks are dissolved, and their charters are returned to the appropriate regulatory agencies. Both banks' shareholders have dissenters' rights.

Consumer

REGULATION E, 12 CFR 205.2 (e)

"A natural person."

REGULATION Z, 12 CFR 226.2 (a) (11)

"A cardholder or a natural person to whom consumer credit is offered or extended. However, for purposes of rescission under Sections 226.15 and 226.23, the term also includes a natural person in whose principal dwelling a security interest is or will be retained or acquired, if that person's ownership interest in the dwelling is or will be subject to the security interest."

Consumer Account

REGULATION CC, 12 CFR 229.2 (n)

"Any account used primarily for personal, family, or household purposes."

Consumer Complaint

REGULATION AA, 12 CFR 227.1 (b)

"An allegation by or on behalf of an individual, group of individuals, or other entity that a particular act or practice of a state member bank is unfair or deceptive, or in violation of a regulation issued by the Board of Governors of the Federal Reserve System pursuant to a federal statute, or in violation of any other act or regulation under which the bank must operate."

Consumer Credit

REGULATION B, 12 CFR 202.2 (h)

"Credit extended to a natural person primarily for personal, family, or household purposes."

REGULATION Z, 12 CFR 226.2 (a) (12)

"Credit offered or extended to a consumer primarily for personal, family, or household purposes."

Consumer Lease

REGULATION M, 12 CFR 213.2 (a) (6)

"A contract in the form of a bailment or lease for the use of personal property by a natural person primarily for personal, family, or household purposes, for a period of time exceeding four months, for a total contractual obligation not exceeding $25,000, whether or not the lessee has the option to purchase or otherwise become the owner of the property at the expiration of the lease. It does not include a lease which meets the definition of a credit sale in Regulation Z, 12 CFR 226.2(a), nor does it include a lease for agricultural, business, or commercial purposes or one made to an organization."

Consummation

REGULATION Z, 12 CFR 226.2 (a) (13)

"The time that a consumer becomes contractually obligated on a credit transaction."

Contiguous Cities, Towns, or Villages

REGULATION L, 12 CFR 212.2 (d)

"Cities, towns, or villages whose borders actually touch each other."

Contingency Reserve

Reserve set aside, representing a specified dollar amount of surplus or undivided profits, to meet unanticipated needs of the bank or a potential, yet unrealized loss. The amount cannot be definitely ascertained.

Contingent Liability

Off-balance-sheet items that are potential liabilities such as loan commitments, lines of credit, letters of credit, foreign exchange contracts, and pending litigation.

Contractually Liable

REGULATION B, 12 CFR 202.2 (i)

"Expressly obligated to repay all debts arising on an account by reason of an agreement to that effect."

Contributed Capital

Representing paid-capital, the payments in cash or property made to a bank or bank holding company by its shareholders in exchange for capital stock.

Control of a Holding Company or Bank

PER REGULATION O, 12 CFR 215.2 (b)

(1) "That a person directly or indirectly, or acting through or in concert with one or more persons

(i) owns, controls, or has the power to vote 25 percent or more of any class of voting securities of the holding company or bank;

(ii) controls in any manner the election of a majority of the directors of the holding company or bank; or

(iii) has the power to exercise a controlling influence over the management or policies of the holding company or bank.

(2) A person is presumed to have control, including the power to exercise a controlling influence over the management or policies of a holding company or bank if

(i) the person is

(A) an executive officer or director of the company or bank and

(B) directly or indirectly owns, controls, or has the power to vote more than 10 percent of any class of voting securities of the holding company or bank; or

(ii)(A) the person directly or indirectly owns, controls, or has the power to vote more than 10 percent of any class of voting securities of the holding company or bank, and

(B) no other person owns, controls, or has the power to vote a greater percentage of that class of voting securities.

(3) An individual is not considered to have control, including the power to exercise a controlling influence over the management or policies, of a holding company or bank solely by virtue of the individual's position as an officer or director of the holding company or bank.

(4) A person may rebut a presumption established by paragraph (b)(2) of this section by submitting to the appropriate federal banking agency (as defined in 12 USC 1813[q]) written materials that, in the agency's judgment, demonstrate an absence of control."

Convertible Security

A security that may be exchanged at the issuer's or holder's option for another class of security, usually common stock. Preferred stocks and bonds also may carry conversion privileges.

Core Deposits

Customer deposit relationships that are based on convenience, financial service, or loyalty versus interest rate paid; deposits that are not rate sensitive.

Corporate Joint Venture

A corporation owned and operated by a group of banks or other businesses (joint venturers), no one of which has a majority interest. It is operated as a separate and specific business or project for the mutual benefit of the joint venturers. Each joint venturer may participate, directly or indirectly, in the management of the joint venture. An entity that is a majority-owned subsidiary of one of the joint venturers is not a corporate joint venture.

Correspondent Bank

A bank that accepts deposits of, and performs banking services for, other depository institutions.

Cosigner

A person who signs for a loan and assumes equal liability for it along with another person.

Coupon Stripping, Treasury Receipts, and STRIPS

Coupon stripping occurs when a security holder physically detaches unmatured coupons from the principal portion of a security and sells either the detached coupons or the ex-coupon security separately. (Such transactions are generally considered by federal bank supervisory agencies to represent "improper investment practices" for banks.)

A variation of coupon stripping has been developed by several securities firms, which have marketed instruments with such names as CATS (Certificates of Accrual on Treasury Securities), TIGR (Treasury Investment Growth Receipts), COUGAR (Certificates on Government Receipts),

LION (Lehman Investment Opportunity Notes), and ETR (East Treasury Receipts).

A securities dealer purchases U.S. Treasury securities, delivers them to a trustee, and sells receipts representing the rights to future interest and/or principal payments on the U.S. Treasury securities held by the trustee. Such Treasury receipts are not an obligation of the government of the United States.

Under a program called Separate Trading of Registered Interest and Principal Securities (STRIPS), the U.S. Treasury has issued certain long-term note and bond issues that are maintained in the book-entry system operated by the Federal Reserve Banks in a manner that permits separate trading and ownership of the interest and principal payments on these issues. Even after the interest or principal portions of U.S. Treasury STRIPS have been separately traded, they remain obligations of the government of the United States, as detailed in the *Consolidated Reports of Condition and Income Instructions*.

Covered Transaction

PER FEDERAL RESERVE ACT SECTION 23A (b) (7)

With respect to an affiliate of a bank that is a member of the Federal Reserve System or a savings loan:

(A) A loan or extension of credit to the affiliate;

(B) A purchase of or an investment in securities issued by the affiliate;

(C) A purchase of assets, including assets subject to an agreement to repurchase, from the affiliate, except such purchase of real and personal property as may be specifically exempted by the Board by order or regulation;

(D) The acceptance of securities issued by the affiliate as collateral security for a loan or extension of credit to any person or company; or

(E) The issuance of a guarantee, acceptance, or letter of credit, including an endorsement or standby letter of credit, on behalf of an affiliate.

Credit

REGULATION B, 12 CFR 202.2 (j)

"The right granted by a creditor to an applicant to defer payment of a debt, incur debt and defer its payment, or purchase property or services and defer payment therefor."

REGULATION E, 12 CFR 205.2 (f)

"The right granted by a financial institution to a consumer to defer payment of debt, incur debt and defer its payment, or purchase property or services and defer payment therefor."

REGULATION Z, 12 CFR 226.2 (a) (14)

"The right to defer payment of debt or to incur debt and defer its payment."

Credit Card

REGULATION B, 12 CFR 202.2 (k)

"Any card, plate, coupon book, or other single credit device that may be used from time to time to obtain money, property, or services on credit."

Regulation Z definition is the same.

Credit Life Insurance

This type of insurance insures payment of the unpaid balance of an outstanding loan upon the death of the individual primarily responsible party for the loan.

Credit Risk

Credit risk includes not only the loss of interest repayment but also the loss of principal. Factors considered in credit risk include lack of repayment according to terms of principal, interest, or timing of payment. It focuses on the probability that a debt will not be repaid.

Credit Sale

REGULATION Z, 12 CFR 226.2(a)(16)

"A sale in which the seller is a creditor. The term includes a bailment or lease (unless terminable without penalty at any time by the consumer) under which the consumer:

(i) Agrees to pay as compensation for use a sum substantially equivalent to, or in excess of, the total value of the property and services involved; and

(ii) Will become (or has the option to become), for no additional consideration or for nominal consideration, the owner of the property upon compliance with the agreement."

Credit Transaction

REGULATION B, 12 CFR 202.2 (m)

"Every aspect of an applicant's dealings with a creditor regarding an application for credit or an existing extension of credit (including, but not limited to, information requirements; investigation procedures; standards of creditworthiness; terms of credit; furnishing of credit information; revocation, alteration, or termination of credit; and collection procedures)."

Creditor

REGULATION B, 12 CFR 202.2 (l)

"A person who, in the ordinary course of business, regularly participates in the decision of whether or not to extend credit. The term includes a creditor's assignee, transferee, or subrogee who so participates. For purposes of Sections 202.4 and 202.5(a) of Regulation B, the term also includes a person who, in the ordinary course of business, regularly refers applicants or prospective applicants to creditors, or selects or offers to select creditors to whom requests for credit may be made. In the event of a violation of this regulation committed by another creditor a person is not a creditor unless the person knows about, or had reasonable notice of, the act, policy, or practice that constituted the violation before becoming involved in the credit transaction. The term does not include a person whose only participation in a credit transaction involves honoring a credit card."

REGULATION Z, 12 CFR 226.2(a)(17)

(1)(i) "A person

(A) who regularly (more than 25 times [or more than 5 times for transactions secured by a dwelling] in the preceding calendar year) extends consumer credit that is subject to a finance charge or is payable by written agreement in more than four installments (not including a downpayment), and

(B) to whom the obligation is initially payable, either on the face of the note or contract, or by agreement when there is no note or contract.

(ii) For purposes of Regulation Z, Sections 226.4(c), 226.9(d), and 226.12(e), a person that honors a credit card is a creditor.

(iii) For purposes of Regulation Z, Subpart B—Open-End Credit, any card issuer that extends either open-end credit or credit that is not subject to a finance charge and is not payable by written agreement in more than four installments.

(iv) For purposes of Regulation Z, Subpart B—Open-End Credit (except for the credit and charge card disclosures contained in sections 226.5[a] and 226.9[e], and [f], the finance-charge disclosures contained in sections 226.6[a] and 226.7[d] through [g] and the right of rescission set forth in Section 226.15), and Subpart C—Closed-End Credit, any card issuer that extends closed-end credit that is subject to a finance charge or is payable in more than four installments is a creditor."

Criticized Assets

Assets rated special mention, substandard, doubtful, or loss. Classified assets include only substandard, doubtful, or loss classified assets. Assets categorized as criticized assets are assets for which the degree of collectibility is of some level of question. *See also* **SUBSTANDARD, DOUBTFUL, or LOSS CLASSIFICATION.**

Cross System Sender Net Debit Cap

Maximum ceiling on the aggregate net debit position that an individual sender of funds can incur at any point during the day.

Cumulative Dividend

A feature of preferred stock that requires all past preferred dividends to be paid before any common dividends are paid.

Cumulative Voting

Method of voting whereby one vote per share is granted each shareholder. For example, a shareholder with ten shares can cast ten votes. The shareholder can allocate his ten votes at will or vote all ten for one director. This feature assures minority shareholders a voice in the control of a company and the voting on corporate issues.

Current Coupon

Interest rate for mortgage-backed securities, generally about fifty basis points less than the most widely quoted interest rate for fixed rate mortgages.

Current Market Value of a Security or Collateral

REGULATION U, 12 CFR 221.2 (d)

"A security means;

(1)(i) if quotations are available, the closing sale price of the security on the preceding business day, as appearing on any regularly published reporting or quotation service; or

(ii) if there is no closing sale price, the bank may use any reasonable estimate of the market value of the security as of the close of business on the preceding business day; or

(iii) if the credit is used to finance the purchase of the security, the total cost of purchase, which may include any commissions charged.

(2) For any other collateral it means a value determined by any reasonable method in accordance with sound banking practices."

Current Yield

Annual interest (or dividends) divided by the current market price of a bond (or stock). For stocks the "annual dividends" figure is the latest quarterly dividend multiplied by four.

Custody Account

An account in which securities or other assets are held by a bank under a safekeeping arrangement with, and on behalf of, a customer .

Customer

REGULATION S, 12 CFR 219.2 (e)

"Any person or authorized representative of that person who utilized or is utilizing any service of a financial institution, or for whom a financial institution is acting or has acted as a fiduciary, in relation to an account maintained in the person's name. 'Customer' does not include corporations or partnerships comprised of more than five persons."

REGULATION U, 12 CFR 221.2 (e)

"Any person or persons acting jointly, to or for whom a bank extends or maintains credit."

D

Date of Payment

Date on which payment of shareholder dividends is made.

Date of Record

Date on which ownership of shares is recognized in terms of who will receive dividends or be eligible to vote shares in an election.

Date of Settlement

PER THE DEPARTMENT OF HOUSING AND URBAN DEVELOPMENT'S
REGULATION X, 24 CFR 3500.2 (a)

The date on which the documents creating the security interest in real property become effective as between the borrower and the lender, except that in the conversion of a construction loan to a permanent security interest in real property to finance purchase by a first user, date of settlement shall be the date on which title is transferred as between the seller and buyer not subject to revocation by seller or buyer.

De Novo Depository Institution

REGULATION D, 12 CFR 204.2 (p)

"A depository institution that was not engaged in business on July 1, 1979, and is not the successor by merger or consolidation to a depository institution that was engaged in business prior to the date of merger or consolidation."

Dealer Activity

Operations within an institution responsible for trading,

dealing, and/or underwriting in securities. To be involved in bank dealer activities does not require the establishment of a separate department.

Dealer Reserve Account

A dealer reserve account arises when a bank purchases at full face value a dealer's installment note receivables, but credits less than the full face value directly to the dealer's account. The remaining amount is credited to a separate dealer reserve account. That account is held by the bank as collateral for the installment notes. The bank will subsequently disburse to the dealer predetermined portions of the reserve as the purchased notes are paid in a timely manner.

Demand Deposit

A deposit payable on demand, or a time deposit with a maturity period or required notice period of less than 14 days, on which the depository institution does not reserve the right to require at least fourteen days' written notice of intended withdrawal. Commonly takes the form of a checking account.

REGULATION D, 12 CFR 204.2 (b)

"A deposit that is payable on demand, or a deposit issued with an original maturity or required notice period of less than seven days, or a deposit representing funds for which the depository institution does not reserve the right to require at least seven days' written notice of an intended withdrawal.

Demand deposits may be in the form of:

(i) checking accounts;

(ii) certified, cashier's and officer's checks (including checks issued by the depository institution in payment of dividends);

(iii) traveler's checks and money orders that are primary obligations of the issuing institution;

(iv) checks or drafts drawn by, or on behalf of, a non-United States office of a depository institution on an account maintained at any of the institution's United States offices;

(v) letters of credit sold for cash or its equivalent;

(vi) withheld taxes, withheld insurance, and other withheld funds;

(vii) time deposits that have matured or time deposits upon which the contractually required notice of withdrawal was given and the notice period has expired and which have not been renewed (either by action of the depositor or automatically under the terms of the deposit agreement); and

(viii) an obligation to pay, on demand or within six days, a check (or other instrument, device, or arrangement for the transfer of funds) drawn on the depository institution, where the account of the institution's customer already has been debited."

The term *demand deposit* also means deposits or accounts on which the depository institution has reserved the right to require at least seven days' written notice prior to withdrawal or transfer of any funds in the account and from which the depositor is authorized to make withdrawals or transfers in excess of the withdrawal or transfer limitations specified in Section 204.2(d)(2) for such an account and the account is not a NOW account, or an ATS account or other account that meets the criteria specified in either Section 204.2(b)(3)(ii) or (iii).

See Regulation D, 12 CFR 204.2(b)(3) for examples of items that are not considered to be demand deposits.

REGULATION Q, 12 CFR 217.2 (a)

"Any deposit that is considered to be a demand deposit under Section 204.2(b) of Regulation D, Reserve Requirements of Depository Institutions (12 CFR 204)."

Demand Draft

A draft that is payable immediately upon presentation to the drawee. This type of draft is also termed a "sight" or "presentation" draft.

Deposit

REGULATION D, 12 CFR 204.2(a)

(1)(i) "The unpaid balance of money or its equivalent received or held by a depository institution in the usual course of business and for which it has given or is obligated to give credit, either conditionally or unconditionally, to an account, including interest credited, or which is evidenced by an instrument on which the depository institution is primarily liable;

(ii) Money received or held by a depository institution, or the credit given for money or its equivalent received or held by the depository institution in the usual course of business for a special or specific purpose, regardless of the legal relationships established thereby, including escrow funds, funds held as security for securities loaned by the depository institution, funds deposited as advance payment on subscriptions to United States government securities, and funds held to meet its acceptances;

(iii) An outstanding draft, cashier's check, money order, or officer's check drawn on the depository institution and issued in the usual course of business for any purpose, including payment for services, dividends, or purchases;

(iv) Any due bill or other liability or undertaking on the part of a depository institution to sell or deliver securities to, or purchase securities for the account of, any customer (including another depository institution), involving either the receipt of funds by the depository institution, regardless of the use of the proceeds, or a debit to an account of the customer before the securities are delivered. A deposit arises thereafter, if after three business days from the date of issuance of the obligation, the depository institution does not fully collateralize its obligation with securities similar to the securities purchased. A security is similar if it is of the same type and if it is of comparable maturity to that purchased by the customer;

(v) Any liability of a depository institution's affiliate that is not a depository institution, on any promissory note, acknowledgement of advance, due bill, or similar obligation (written or oral), with a maturity of less than one and one-half years, to the extent that the proceeds are used to supply or to maintain the availability of funds (other than capital) to the depository institution, except any such obligation that, had it been issued directly by the depository institution, would not constitute a deposit. If an obligation of an affiliate of a depository institution is regarded as a deposit and is used to purchase assets from the depository institution, the maturity of the deposit is determined by the shorter of the maturity of the obligation issued or the remaining maturity of the assets purchased. If the proceeds from an affiliate's obligation are placed in the depository institution in the form of a reservable deposit, no reserves need be maintained against the obligation of the affiliate since reserves are required to be maintained against the deposit issued by the depository institution. However, the maturity of the deposit issued to the affiliate shall be the shorter of the maturity of the affiliate's obligation or the maturity of the deposit;

(vi) Credit balances;

(vii) Any liability of a depository institution on any promissory note, acknowledgement of advance, banker's acceptance, or similar obligation (written or oral), including mortgage-backed bonds, that is issued or undertaken by a depository institution as a means of obtaining funds, except any such obligation that

(A) is issued or undertaken and held for the account of

(1) an office located in the United States of another depository institution, foreign bank, Edge or agreement corporation, or New York Investment (Article XII) Company;

(2) the United States government or any agency thereof; or

(3) the Export-Import Bank of the United States, Minbanc Capital Corporation, the Government Development Bank for Puerto Rico, a Federal Reserve Bank, a Federal Home Loan Bank, or the National Credit Union Administration Central Liquidity Facility;

(B) arises from a transfer of direct obligations of, or obligations that are fully guaranteed as to principal and interest by, the United States government or any agency thereof that the depository institution is obligated to repurchase;

(C) is not insured by a federal agency, is subordinated to the claims of depositors, has a weighted average maturity of seven years or more, and is issued by a depository institution with the approval of, or under the rules and regulations of, its primary federal supervisor;

(D) arises from a borrowing by a depository institution from a dealer in securities, for one business day, of proceeds of a transfer of deposit credit in a Federal Reserve Bank or other immediately available funds, (commonly referred to as federal funds), received by such dealer on the date of the loan in connection with clearance of securities transactions; or

(E) arises from the creation, discount, and subsequent sale by a depository institution of its banker's acceptance of the type described in paragraph 7 of Section 13 of the Federal Reserve Act (12 USC 372);

(viii) Any liability of a depository institution that arises from the creation after June 20, 1983, of a banker's acceptance that is not of the type described in paragraph 7 of Section 13 of the Federal Reserve Act (12 USC 372) except any such liability held for the account of an entity specified in 12 CFR 204.2(a)(1)(vii)(A)."

See 12 CFR 204.2(a)(2) for examples of items that are not considered to be "deposits" under Regulation D.

REGULATION Q, 12 CFR 217.2 (b)

"Any liability of a member bank that is considered to be a 'deposit' under Section 204.2(a) of the Board's Regulation D, Reserve Requirements of Depository Institutions (12 CFR 204)."

Depository Bank

PER REGULATION CC, 12 CFR 229.2 (o)

The first bank to which a check is transferred even though it is also the paying bank or the payee. A check deposited in an account is deemed to be transferred to the bank holding the account into which the check is deposited, even though the check is physically received and endorsed first by another bank.

Depository Holding Company

REGULATION L, 12 CFR 212.2(e)

"A bank holding company or a savings and loan holding company (as more fully defined in Section 202 of the Interlocks Act) having its principal office located in the United States."

Depository Institution

REGULATION A, 12 CFR 201.2 (a)

(1) An institution that maintains reservable transaction accounts or nonpersonal time deposits and is:

(A) "an insured bank as defined in Section 3 of the Federal Deposit Insurance Act (12 USC 1813[h] or a bank that is eligible to apply to become an insured bank under Section 5 of such Act (12 USC 1815);

(B) a savings bank or mutual savings bank as defined in Section 3 of the Federal Deposit Insurance Act (12 USC 1813[f], [g]);

(C) an insured credit union as defined in Section 101 of the Federal Credit Union Act (12 USC 1752[7]) or a credit union that is eligible to become an insured credit union under section 201 of such Act (12 USC 1781);

(D) a member as defined in Section 2 of the Federal Home Loan Bank Act (12 USC 1422[4]); or

(E) an insured institution as defined in Section 401 of the National Housing Act (12 USC 1724[a]) or an institution that is eligible to apply to become an insured institution under Section 403 of such Act (12 USC 1726).

(2) A financial institution that is not required to maintain reserves under Regulation D (12 CDR 204) because it is organized solely to do business with other financial institutions, is owned primarily by the financial institutions with

which it does business, and does not do business with the general public is not a depository institution."

PER REGULATION D, 12 CFR 204.2 (m)

(1)(i) "Any insured bank as defined in Section 3 of the Federal Deposit Insurance Act (12 USC 1813[h]) or any bank that is eligible to apply to become an insured bank under Section 5 of such Act (12 USC 1815);

(ii) any savings bank or mutual savings bank as defined in Section 3 of the Federal Deposit Insurance Act (12 USC 1813[f], [g]);

(iii) any insured credit union as defined in Section 101 of the Federal Credit Union Act (12 USC 1752[7]) or any credit union that is eligible to apply to become an insured credit union under Section 201 of such Act (12 USC 1781);

(iv) any member as defined in Section 2 of the Federal Home Loan Bank Act (12 USC 1422[4]); and

(v) any insured institution as defined in Section 401 of the National Housing Act (12 USC 1724[a]) or any institution which is eligible to apply to become an insured institution under Section 403 of such Act (12 USC 1726).

(2) 'Depository institution' does not include international organizations such as the World Bank, the Inter-American Development Bank, and the Asian Development Bank."

REGULATION J, 12 CFR 210.2 (l) (1)

"A depository institution as defined in section 19(b) of the Federal Reserve Act (12 USC 461[b])."

REGULATION L, 12 CFR 212.2 (f)

"A commercial bank (including a private bank), a savings bank, a trust company, a savings and loan association, a building and loan association, a homestead association, a cooperative bank, an industrial bank, or a credit union, chartered in the United States and having a principal office located in the United States. Additionally, a United States office, including a branch or agency, of a foreign commercial bank is a 'depository institution'."

The Depository Institutions Deregulation and Monetary Control Act of 1980 (MCA)

Among its major provisions, this act applied uniform reserve requirements to all depository institutions with certain types of accounts and required reports from these depository institutions. It also extended access to the Federal Reserve discount window and to other Federal Reserve services in step with the implementation of a fee schedule.

Depository Organization

REGULATION L, 12 CFR 212.2 (g)

"A depository institution or a depository holding company."

Direct Investment

Equity investment by an institution in ventures such as real estate development and business, versus traditional debt investment. With direct investment, an institution gains ownership interest in the venture rather than loaning money to finance it. Specific regulatory statutes and rulings exist governing such investments.

Directly Incurred Costs

REGULATION S, 12 CFR 219.2 (f)

"Costs incurred solely and necessarily as a consequence of searching for, reproducing, or transporting books, papers, records, or other data, in order to comply with legal process or a formal written request or a customer's authorization to produce a customer's financial records. The term does not include any allocation of fixed costs (overhead, equipment, depreciation, etc.). If a financial institution has financial records that are stored at an independent storage facility that charges a fee to search for, reproduce, or transport particular records requested, these costs are considered to be directly incurred by the financial institution."

Directly or Indirectly

REGULATION K, 12 CFR 211.2 (c)

"When used in reference to activities or investments of an organization means activities or investments of the organization or of any subsidiary of the organization."

Director of a Member Bank

REGULATION O, 12 CFR 215.2 (c)

(1) "Any director of a member bank, whether or not receiving compensation,

(2) Any director of a bank holding company (as defined in 12 USC 1841[a]) of which the member bank is a subsidiary, and

(3) Any director of any other subsidiary of that bank holding company."

An advisory director is not considered a director if the advisory director:

1. is not elected by the shareholders of the company or bank,

2. is not authorized to vote on matters before the board of directors, and

3. provides solely general policy advice to the board of directors.

Directors' and Officers' (D&O) Insurance

Insurance coverage purchased by institutions, which protects directors and officers against personal liability for losses incurred by the institution due to an individual's negligent performance as an officer or director.

Discount

A discount arises when a bank purchases a security, loan, or other asset at a price below its par or face value, typically because the current level of interest rates for such assets is greater than its contract or stated rate of interest. A discount is also present on instruments that do not have a stated rate of interest such as U.S. Treasury bills and commercial paper. The difference between the par or face value and the purchase price represents the discount that all banks on the accrual basis of accounting are required to accrete.

Discount Brokerage Activity

Operations of a brokerage business, undertaken by a financial institution, where orders are executed to buy or sell securities at a commission rate much less than those charged by a full-service broker. Different levels of service may be offered; however, discount brokerage operations do not offer investment advice to clients.

Discount Rate

The interest rate at which eligible depository institutions may borrow funds, usually for short periods, directly from the Federal Reserve Banks. The law requires the board of directors of each Reserve Bank to establish the discount rate every fourteen days subject to the approval of the board of governors.

Discriminate Against an Applicant

REGULATION B, 12 CFR 202.2 (n)

"To treat an applicant less favorably than other applicants in reference to an extension of credit."

Dividend

Payout of current or retained earnings to shareholders of an institution in the form of cash or stock; in certain instances, property is dividend to the parent holding company. Dividends are declared by the Board of Directors on a periodic (quarterly, semiannually or annually) basis, with each shareholder receiving the declared amount per share owned.

Documentary Draft

A draft to which documents are attached, which is delivered

to the drawee when he or she accepts or pays the draft, and which ordinarily controls title to the merchandise.

Domestic Office

For Call Report purposes, a domestic office of the reporting bank is a branch or subsidiary (other than an Edge or Agreement subsidiary) located in the fifty states of the United States or the District of Columbia, or a branch on a U.S. military facility, wherever located. The domestic offices of the reporting bank exclude all International Banking Facilities (IBFs); all offices of Edge and Agreement subsidiaries, including their U.S. offices; and all branches and other subsidiaries of a bank located in Puerto Rico, U.S. territories and possessions, or foreign countries.

Domicile

Domicile is used to determine the foreign (non-U.S. addressee) or domestic (U.S. addressee) status of a customer of a bank for the purpose of reporting in the bank's Report of Condition and Income. Domicile is determined by the principal residence address of an individual or the principal business address of a corporation, partnership, or sole proprietorship.

Doubtful Classification

Rating assigned to assets that have all the weaknesses associated with those assets classified substandard with the added characteristics that the weaknesses make collection in full, on the basis of currently existing values, conditions, or facts, improbable and questionable.

Downpayment

REGULATION Z, 12 CFR 226.2 (a) (18)

"An amount, including the value of any property used as a trade-in, paid to a seller to reduce the cash price of goods or services purchased in a credit sale transaction. A deferred portion of a downpayment may be treated as part of the downpayment if it is payable not later than the due date of the second otherwise regularly scheduled payment and is not subject to a finance charge."

Draft

A draft is an order in writing signed by one party (the drawer) requesting a second party (the drawee) to make payment in lawful money at a determinable future time to a third party (the payee). Drafts occasionally may be written to be non-negotiable, in that they will not meet all the requirements of the Uniform Negotiable Instruments Act. Drafts generally arise from a commercial transaction, whereby the seller makes an agreement with a buyer in advance for the transfer of goods. The draft may be made out by the seller (the drawer) ordering the buyer (the drawee) to pay his or her bank (the payee) for the goods purchased. It may be accompanied by a bill of lading, which the bank will surrender to the buyer upon payment of the draft. The buyer may then claim the goods at the office of the carrier that transported them to the buyer's place of business.

Drafts may be classified as to time element, such as sight or presentation drafts. A time draft is presented at sight, accepted, and then paid on the agreed-upon date, which may be 30, 60, 90, days or longer after presentation and acceptance.

Due Bill

An obligation that results when a bank sells an asset and receives payment, but does not deliver the security or other asset. A due bill can also result from a promise to deliver an asset in exchange for value received. In both cases, the receipt of the payment creates an obligation regardless of whether the due bill is issued in written form.

Duration

Average time elapsing before cash flow is received; generally a time element considered in identifying interest rate risk. Calculated generally in terms of weighted average number of periods, i.e., years, until cash flows occur, where the relative present values of each receipt are used as weights.

Dwelling

REGULATION Z, 12 CFR 226.2 (a) (19)

"A residential structure that contains one to four units, whether or not that structure is attached to real property. The term includes an individual condominium unit, cooperative unit, mobile home, and trailer, if it is used as a residence."

E

Edge Corporation

A federally chartered corporation organized under Section 25(a) of the Federal Reserve Act and subject to Federal Reserve Regulation K, 12 CFR 211. Edge corporations are allowed to engage only in international banking or other financial transactions related to international business.

Elderly

REGULATION B, 12 CFR 202.2 (o)

"Age 62 or older."

Electronic Fund Transfer (EFT)

REGULATION E, 12 CFR 205.2 (g)

"Any transfer of funds, other than a transaction originated by check, draft, or similar paper instrument, that is initiated through an electronic terminal, telephone, or computer or magnetic tape for the purpose of ordering, instructing, or authorizing a financial institution to debit or credit an account. The term includes, but is not limited to, point-of-sale transfers, automated teller machine transfers, direct deposits or withdrawals of funds, and transfers initiated by telephone. It includes all transfers resulting from debit card transactions, including those that do not involve an electronic terminal at the time of the transaction. The term does not include payments made by check, draft, or similar instrument at an electronic terminal."

Electronic Fund Transfer Systems (EFTS)

A variety of systems and technologies for transferring funds (money) electronically rather than by check. Includes Fedwire, Bankwire, automated clearinghouses (ACHs), and other automated systems.

Electronic Payment

REGULATION CC, 12 CFR 229.2 (p)

"A wire transfer or an automated clearinghouse (ACH) credit transfer."

Electronic Terminal

REGULATION E, 12 CFR 205.2 (h)

"An electronic device, other than a telephone operated by a consumer, through which a consumer may initiate an electronic fund transfer. The term includes, but is not limited to, point-of-sale terminals, automated teller machines, and cash dispensing machines."

Embezzlement

Fraudulent use or misapplication of funds to one's own accounts, fraudulent use of funds or other property that has been lawfully entrusted to one's care.

Empirically Derived and Other Credit Scoring Systems

REGULATION B, 12 CFR 202.2 (p)

"A credit scoring system is a system that evaluates an applicant's creditworthiness mechanically, based on key attributes of the applicant and aspects of the transaction, and that determines, alone or in conjunction with an evaluation of additional information about the applicant, whether an applicant is deemed creditworthy. To qualify as an empirically derived, demonstrably and statistically sound, credit scoring system, the system must be:

(i) based on data that are derived from an empirical comparison of sample groups or the population of creditworthy and noncreditworthy applicants who applied for credit within a reasonable preceding period of time;

(ii) developed for the purpose of evaluating the credit-worthiness of applicants with respect to the legitimate business interests of the creditor utilizing the system (including, but not limited to, minimizing bad debt losses and operating expenses in accordance with the creditor's business judgment);

(iii) developed and validated using accepted statistical principles and methodology; and

(iv) periodically revalidated by the use of appropriate statistical principles and methodology and adjusted as necessary to maintain predictive ability."

Part Two, 12 CFR 202.2(p)(2), of the regulation's definition describes under what conditions a creditor may use an empirically derived, demonstrably and statistically sound credit scoring system obtained from another person.

Employee Retirement Income Security Act (ERISA)

An acronym for the Employee Retirement Income Security Act of 1974, which established federal minimum standards for employee benefit plans, including those regulating the conduct of plan fiduciaries and trustees. The act also established an insurance program designed to guarantee workers receipt of pension benefits if their defined benefit pension plan should terminate.

Engaged in Banking

REGULATION K, 12 CFR 211.2 (d)

"In referring to an Edge corporation, it is 'engaged in banking' if it is ordinarily engaged in the business of accepting deposits in the United States from nonaffiliated persons."

Engaged in Business (or Engaged in Activities) in the U.S.

REGULATION K, 12 CFR 211.2 (e)

"Maintaining and operating an office (other than a representative office) or subsidiary in the U.S."

Equity Capital

The investments made by shareholders in an organization.

Eurocurrency

The nonresident ownership of one of the major western European currencies. Eurocurrencies, similar to Eurodollars, are frequently available for borrowing in the London exchange markets.

Eurocurrency Liabilities

REGULATION D, 12 CFR 204.2 (h)

(1) "For a depository institution or an Edge or agreement corporation organized under the laws of the United States, the sum, if positive, of the following:

(i) net balances due to its non-United States offices and its international banking facilities ('IBFs') from its United States offices;

(ii)(A) for a depository institution organized under the laws of the United States, assets (including participations) acquired from its United States offices and held by its non-United States offices, by its IBF, or by non-United States offices of an affiliated Edge or agreement corporation; or

(B) for an Edge or agreement corporation, assets (including participations) acquired from its United States offices and held by its non-United States offices, by its IBF, by non-United States offices of its U.S. or foreign parent institution, or by non-United States offices of an affiliated Edge or agreement corporation; and

(iii) credit outstanding from its non-United States offices to United States residents (other than assets acquired and net balances due from its United States offices), except credit extended

(A) from its non-United States offices in the aggregate amount of $100,000 or less to any United States resident,

(B) by a non-United States office that at no time during the computation period had credit outstanding to United States residents exceeding $1 million,

(C) to an international banking facility, or

(D) to an institution that will be maintaining reserves on such credit pursuant to this part. Credit extended from non-United States offices or from IBFs to a foreign branch, office, subsidiary, affiliate, or other foreign establishment ('foreign affiliate') controlled by one or more domestic corporations is not regarded as credit extended to a United States resident if the proceeds will be used to finance the operations outside the United States of the borrower or of other foreign affiliates of the controlling domestic corporation(s).

(2) For a United States branch or agency of a foreign bank, the sum, if positive, of the following:

(i) net balances due to its foreign bank (including offices thereof located outside the United States) and its international banking facility after deducting an amount equal to 8 percent of the following: the United States branch's or agency's total assets less the sum of

(A) cash items in process of collection;

(B) unposted debits;

(C) demand balances due from depository institutions organized under the laws of the United States and from other foreign banks;

(D) balances due from foreign central banks; and

(E) positive net balances due from its IBF, its foreign bank, and the foreign bank's United States and non-United States offices; and

(ii) assets (including participations) acquired from the United States branch or agency (other than assets required to be sold by federal or state supervisory authorities) and held by its foreign bank (including offices thereof located outside the United States), by its parent holding company, by non-United States offices or an IBF of an affiliated Edge or agreement corporation, or by its IBFs."

Eurodollars

Deposits denominated in U.S. dollars at banks and other financial institutions outside the United States. Although this name originated because of the large amounts of such deposits held at banks in Western Europe, similar deposits in other parts of the world are also called Eurodollars or Asian Dollars.

Examination

On-site and off-site examinations are conducted by state or federal regulatory authorities to assess the condition and performance of financial institutions, the quality of their operations, the capacity of management, and to enforce compliance with state and federal laws. All facets of the examination focus on ultimately determining the liquidity and solvency—present and future—and the legality of the financial institution acts including the actions of its board of directors, management, and staff.

Examination Control

The process whereby examiners control the institution records, work papers, and related elements during an examination to ensure effectiveness and efficiency. The examiner-in-charge (EIC) is primarily responsible for this function.

Examination Scope

Identified activities to be performed during the examination to meet the objectives stated in the regulatory agency plan or strategy for that institution, and the regulatory handbook for that agency. The scope determines the level of procedures performed and the types of procedures.

Examiner

Employees of a regulatory agency charged with the responsibility of performing examination procedures; writing examination reports; assessing financial institution safety and soundness, compliance with law, and future prospects; as well as performing other tasks and assignments supportive of the regulatory agency's missions and objectives. Generally, examiners within an agency are assigned different titles based upon experience, recognized performance, and, in certain agencies, the passing of certification tests.

Examiner-in-Charge (EIC)

Also known as head examiner or crew chief, responsible for managing the on-site examination efforts of an examination crew and generally responsible for assigning final ratings to the institution as well as writing the report of examination which will, in turn, be submitted to the board of directors of that institution.

Executive Officer

REGULATION O, 12 CFR 215.2 (d)

"Of a company or bank means a person who participates or has authority to participate (other than in the capacity of a director) in major policy-making functions of the company or bank, whether or not:

(1) the officer has an official title,

(2) the title designates the officer an assistant, or

(3) the officer is serving without salary or other compensation.

The chairman of the board, the president, every vice president, the cashier, the secretary, and the treasurer of a company or bank are considered executive officers, unless

(1) the officer is excluded, by resolution of the board of directors or by the bylaws of the bank or company, from participation (other than in the capacity of a director) in major policy-making functions of the bank or company, and

(2) the officer does not actually participate therein.

For the purpose of Sections 215.4 and 215.7 of Regulation O, an executive officer of a member bank includes an executive officer of

(1) a bank holding company (as defined in 12 USC 1841[a]) of which the member bank is a subsidiary, and

(2) any other subsidiary of that bank holding company, unless the executive officer of the subsidiary

(i) is excluded (by name or by title) from participation in major policy-making functions of the member bank by resolutions of the boards of directors of both the subsidiary and the member bank, and

(ii) does not actually participate in such major policy-making functions."

Extension of Credit

REGULATION B, 12 CFR 202.2 (q)

"The granting of credit in any form including, but not limited to, credit granted in addition to any existing credit or credit limit; credit granted pursuant to an open-end credit plan; the refinancing or other renewal of credit, including the issuance of a new credit card in place of an expiring credit card or in substitution for an existing credit card; the consolidation of two or more obligations or the continuance of existing credit without any special effort to collect at or after maturity."

Extraordinary Items

For Call Report purposes, extraordinary items are material events and transactions that are (1) unusual and (2) infrequent. Both of these conditions must exist in order for an event or transaction to be reported as an extraordinary item.

To be unusual, an event or transaction must be highly abnormal or clearly unrelated to the ordinary and typical activities of banks. An event or transaction that is beyond management's control is not automatically considered to be unusual.

To be infrequent, an event or transaction should not reasonably be expected to recur in the foreseeable future. Although the past occurrence of an event or transaction provides a basis for estimating the likelihood of its future occurrence, the absence of a past occurrence does not automatically imply that an event or transaction is infrequent.

Also refer to APB Opinion No. 30, "Reporting the Results of Operations," which provides further information on treatment of such transactions.

F

Fails

When a bank has sold a security or an asset and does not deliver the security or other asset on the settlement date and does not receive payment, a sales fail exists. When a bank has purchased a security or other asset and does not receive the asset on settlement date and does not pay for it, a purchase fail exists.

Federal Advisory Council (FAC)

This group consists of one member from each Federal Reserve District (usually a banker) elected annually by the Federal Reserve Board of Directors from each of the twelve Federal Reserve Banks. They meet with the board to discuss business and financial conditions and make advisory recommendations.

Federal Deposit Insurance Corporation (FDIC)

Agency of the federal government that insures accounts at most financial institutions. The FDIC also has primary federal supervisory authority over insured state banks that are not members of the Federal Reserve System.

Federal Financial Institutions Examination Council (FFIEC)

Members consist of the Board of Governors of the Federal Reserve System, Federal Deposit Insurance Corporation, Federal Home Loan Bank Board, National Credit Union Administration, and the Office of the Comptroller of the Currency.

Federal Funds

Excess funds held by the Federal Reserve Bank, which depository institutions lend each other, usually on an overnight basis. In addition, federal funds include certain other kinds of borrowings by depository institutions from each other and from federal agencies.

Federal Home Loan Bank System

Financial network established to supply the credit needs and reserves for savings and loans, cooperative banks, and other types of mortgage lenders, in a support similar to the Federal Reserve System. Federal Home Loan Bank System is comprised of twelve regional Federal Home Loan Banks. Money is raised by issuing securities, i.e., notes, bonds, and lending money to S&Ls, based on collateral provided by that institution.

Federal Home Loan Mortgage Corporation (FHLMC)

A government organization established to create a secondary market in conventional mortgages. FHLMC purchases mortgages from federally insured financial institutions and resells them in the form of mortgage-backed, pass-through certificates. All income on securities issued by the FHLMC is subject to federal, state, and local taxation.

Federal Housing Authority (FHA)

A government agency responsible to the Department of Housing and Urban Development, the FHA was formed to carry out the provisions of the National Housing Act approved June 27, 1934. The FHA promotes the ownership of homes and the renovation and remodeling of residences through government-guaranteed loans to homeowners. It insures residential mortgages.

Federal Land Bank (FLB)

The twelve Federal Land Banks, responsible to the Farm Credit Administration, make loans to farmers for the purchase and development of land, equipment, or stock. Those loans are secured by first mortgages on rural real estate. Maturities range from a few months to fifteen years, and bonds maturing in under five years are issued in coupon form only. Longer bonds may be registered if desired. Consolidated Federal Farm Loan bonds are the joint and several obligations of the twelve banks. Although those bonds are not government obligations and are not guaranteed by the government, they are the secured obligations of banks operating under federal charter with governmental supervision. They are issued in denominations of $1,000, $5,000, $10,000, $50,000 and $100,000, and in recent years have not been callable prior to maturity.

Federal National Mortgage Association (Fannie Mae)

The Federal National Mortgage Association is a government-sponsored corporation established by Congress in 1938, owned entirely by private stockholders to serve as a secondary market for Federal Housing Administration, Veterans Administration, or Farmers Home Administration insured or guaranteed mortgages. The association provides liquidity on mortgage investments by buying mortgages from financial institutions, such as savings and loan associations and life insurance companies, when investment funds are in short supply and selling mortgages when funds are plentiful. To finance its operations, Fannie Mae issues debentures, bonds, and common stock, the latter being bought by institutions who sell mortgages to Fannie Mae, as well as by private investors. FNMA stock is listed on the New York Stock Exchange. The bonds and debentures are highly liquid investments that enjoy an active secondary market and have varying maturities up to twenty-five years. Fannie Maes come in bearer form only, in amounts of $10,000 up to $500,000. The maturities on those securities vary and interest is paid semiannually by coupon.

Federal Open Market Committee (FOMC)

A twelve member committee consisting of the seven members of the Federal Reserve Board and five of the twelve Federal Reserve Bank presidents. The president of the Federal Reserve Bank of New York is a permanent member while the other Federal Reserve presidents serve on a rotating basis. The committee sets objectives for the growth of money and credit that are implemented through purchases and sales of U.S. government securities in the open market. The FOMC also establishes policy relating to Federal Reserve System operations in the foreign exchange markets.

Federal Reserve Bank Stock

REGULATION H, 12 CFR 208.2 (e)

"Includes the deposit that may be made with a Federal Reserve Bank in lieu of a subscription for stock by a mutual savings bank which is not permitted to purchase stock in a Federal Reserve Bank, unless otherwise indicated."

Federal Reserve Board (FRB)

Seven governing members of the Federal Reserve System, appointed by the President of the United States for fourteen-year terms. Board members, decisions include determining the country's monetary policy.

Federal Reserve System

The central bank of the United States, created by Congress and consisting of a seven-member Board of Governors in Washington, D.C., twelve regional Reserve Banks, and depository institutions that are subject to reserve requirements. All national banks are members; state chartered banks may elect to become members, and state members are supervised by the Board of Governors and the Reserve Banks. Reserve requirements established by the Federal Reserve Board apply to nonmember depository institutions as well as member banks. Both classes of institutions have access to Federal

Reserve discount borrowing privileges and Federal Reserve services on an equal basis.

Federal Reserve Wire Network (Fed Wire)

High-speed communications system operated by the Federal Reserve System for transferring funds and ownership of book-entry securities between banks. The wire is used to move bank reserves and to make credit available to participants without delay.

Federally Related Mortgage Loan

REGULATION C, 12 CFR 203.2 (d)

"Any loan (other than temporary financing such as a construction loan) secured by a first lien on a one- to four-family dwelling (including a condominium, a cooperative, or a mobile or manufactured home):

(1) that is originated by a federally insured or regulated institution;

(2) that is insured, guaranteed, or supplemented by any federal agency; or

(3) that the originator intends to sell to the Federal National Mortgage Association, the Government National Mortgage Association, or the Federal Home Loan Mortgage Corporation."

Federally Sponsored Lending Agency

An agency or corporation that has been chartered, authorized, or organized as a result of federal legislation for the purpose of providing credit services to a designated sector of the economy. These agencies include Banks for Cooperatives, Federal Home Loan Banks, the Federal Home Loan Mortgage Corporation, Federal Intermediate Credit Banks, Federal Land Banks, the Federal National Mortgage Association, and the Student Loan Marketing Association.

Field Manager

Term generally used by a regulatory agency to designate a field supervisor for field examiners. Different agencies may use different terminology.

Financial Institution

REGULATION C, 12 CFR 203.2 (e)

1. (i) "A commercial bank, savings bank, savings and loan association, building and loan association, homestead association (including a cooperative bank), or credit union that originates federally related mortgage loans;

(ii) A mortgage banking subsidiary of a savings and loan holding company, or a mortgage banking subsidiary of a bank holding company; however, a subsidiary is not a 'mortgage banking subsidiary' under this section of the regulation unless, in the preceding calendar year, 10 percent or more of its loan volume, measured in dollars, consisted of home purchase loans; or

(iii) A savings and loan service corporation that originates or purchases mortgage loans, other than a savings and loan service corporation identified in paragraph (e)(2) of this definition.

2. A majority-owned subsidiary of a financial institution, including a majority-owned savings and loan service corporation, is deemed to be part of the parent institution for purposes of Regulation C."

REGULATION S, 12 CFR 219.2 (a)

"Any office of a bank, savings bank, card issuer as defined in Section 103 of the Consumer Protection Act (15 USC 1602[n]), industrial loan company, trust company, savings and loan, building and loan, or homestead association (including cooperative banks), credit union, or consumer finance institution, located in any state or territory of the United States, the District of Columbia, Puerto Rico, Guam, American Samoa, or the Virgin Islands."

Financial Record

REGULATION S, 12 CFR 219.2 (b)

"An original of, a copy of, or information known to have been derived from, any record held by a financial institution pertaining to a customer's relationship with the financial institution."

Floor Plan Lending

Type of lending whereby retail goods inventory (excluding automobiles) financing is advanced in which each loan advance is secured by inventory. The borrower or dealer borrows to buy inventory, with loan advances required to pay for each inventory purchase, which in turn is pledged as collateral under a trust receipt or other security agreement. Sale proceeds from the sale of inventory in turn is generally applied to the loan outstandings. Out-of-trust situations are those where a dealer sells inventory but does not repay the floor plan advance securing the sold inventory.

Foreign Bank

This term covers all branches of banks chartered and headquartered in foreign countries (including foreign banks owned by U.S. nationals and institutions), including their U.S. domiciled branches and agencies but excluding the foreign branches of U.S. banks. In contrast, the term *banks in foreign countries* covers foreign domiciled branches of banks, including the foreign branches of U.S. banks but excluding the U.S. branches and agencies of foreign banks.

REGULATION D, 12 CFR 204.2 (o)

"Any bank or other similar institution organized under the laws of any country other than the United States or organized under the laws of Puerto Rico, Guam, American Samoa, the Virgin Islands, or other territory or possession of the United States."

PER REGULATION K, 12 CFR 211.2 (g)

"An organization that is organized under the laws of a foreign country, engages in the business of banking, is recognized as a bank by the bank supervisory or monetary authority of the country of its organization or principal banking operations, receives deposits to a substantial extent in the regular course of its business, and has the power to accept demand deposits."

REGULATION Q, 12 CFR 217.2 (c)

"Any bank that is considered to be a 'foreign bank' under section 204.2(o) of the Board's Regulation D, Reserve Requirements of Depository Institutions (12 CFR 204)."

Foreign Branch

REGULATION K, 12 CFR 211.2 (h)

"An office of an organization (other than a representative office) that is located outside the country under the laws of which the organization is established, at which a banking or financing business is conducted."

Foreign Correspondent

REGULATION J, 12 CFR 210.2 (l) (4)

"Any of the following, for which a Reserve Bank maintains an account: a foreign bank or banker, a foreign state as defined in Section 25(b) of the Federal Reserve Act (12 USC 632), or a foreign correspondent or agency referred to in Section 14(e) of that act (12 USC 358)."

Foreign Country

REGULATION K, 12 CFR 211.2 (f)

"Refers to one or more foreign nations, and includes the overseas territories, dependencies, and insular possessions of those nations and of the United States, and the Commonwealth of Puerto Rico."

Foreign Currency Transactions

Transactions occurring in the ordinary course of business (for example, purchases, sales, borrowings, lendings, forward exchange contracts) denominated in currencies other than the office's functional currency. Functional currency is the currency of the primary economic environment in which an office operates. For most banks, the functional currency will be the U.S. dollar. However, if a bank has foreign offices, one or more foreign offices may have a functional currency other than the U.S. dollar.

Foreign Exchange

Simply stated, foreign money. In addition to currency and coin, foreign exchange includes bank assets and liabilities payable in foreign currencies. Also, the trading in or exchange of a foreign currency in relation to another currency. Rates of exchange are established and quoted for various foreign currencies based on the demand, supply, and stability of the currency. Foreign exchange is the means by which values are established for foreign merchandise, thus permitting the exchange of commodities between countries.

Foreign Governments and Official Institutions

Central, state, provincial, and local governments in foreign countries and their ministries, departments, and agencies. These include treasuries, ministries of finance, central banks, developmental banks, exchange control offices, stabilization funds, diplomatic establishments, fiscal agents, and nationalized banks and other banking institutions that are owned by central governments and that have as an important part of their function activities similar to those of a treasury, central bank, exchange control office, or stabilization fund. Also included as foreign official institutions are international, regional, and treaty organizations, such as the International Monetary Fund, the International Bank for Reconstruction and Development (World Bank), the Bank for International Settlements, the Inter-American Development Bank, and the United Nations.

Forward Collection

REGULATION CC, 12 CFR 229.2 (q)

"The process by which a bank sends a check on a cash basis to the paying bank for payment."

Fraud

Intentional misrepresentation of a material fact by one or more persons or organizations in order to secure unfair or unlawful gain.

Futures Contracts and Forward Contracts

Both futures and forward contracts are commitments for delayed delivery of securities or money market instruments, in which the buyer agrees to purchase, and the seller agrees to deliver a specified instrument at a specified price or yield and on a specified future date.

Futures contracts are standardized and are traded on organized exchanges. Exchanges in the U.S. are registered with and regulated by the Commodity Futures Trading Commission.

Forward contracts are traded over the counter, and their terms are not standardized. Such contracts can only be terminated, other than by receipt of the underlying asset, by agreement of both buyer and seller.

G

Gap

The imbalance between fixed-yield assets and fixed-yield liabilities. In *foreign exchange* transactions, it is the period between the maturities for purchases and those for sales of each foreign currency (exchange gap). In *money market* transactions, it is the period between the maturities of placements (loans) and the maturities of borrowings (deposits) of each currency (money market gap). The former occurs when a currency is purchased against one currency and sold against another, each time for different maturities. The money market gap is created by lending an amount of a certain currency for a longer or shorter period than that for which the same currency is borrowed. Mismatched maturities in liabilities, if not properly managed, may cause significant expense in acquiring liquid funds (sale of securities, purchasing federal funds, borrowing) to meet maturing liabilities. Conversely, if assets mature before corresponding liabilities, income may be lost if the funds cannot be reinvested in instruments with equivalent rates.

Garnishment

A writ from a court instructing an employer to withhold all or a part of an employee's wages and to pay these funds to the court or to a plaintiff in a civil action (to whom the employee has an outstanding debt) until the debt is paid.

General Obligation Bonds

State or municipal obligations (debt instruments) backed by the general taxing and borrowing authority of the state or municipality.

Good Faith

REGULATION B, 12 CFR 202.2 (r)

"Honesty in fact in the conduct or transaction."

REGULATION U, 12 CFR 221.2 (f)

"With respect to

(1) the loan value of collateral, means that amount (not exceeding 100 percent of the current market value of the collateral) which a bank, exercising sound judgment, would lend, without regard to the customer's other assets held as collateral in connection with unrelated transactions;

(2) accepting notice or certification from or on behalf of a customer means that the bank or its duly authorized representative is alert to the circumstances surrounding the credit, and if in possession of information that would cause a prudent person not to accept the notice or certification without inquiry, investigates and is satisfied that it is truthful."

Goodwill

Under purchase accounting, the excess of purchase price paid for an asset over its market value. The excess amount generally represents the present value of expected future income flow in excess of a normal return on the investment. Accounting industry and regulatory agencies have very specific guidelines regarding treatment of goodwill.

Government Authority

REGULATION S, 12 CFR 219.2 (c)

"Any agency or department of the United States, or any officer, employee, or agency thereof."

Grandfathered Activities

Activities prohibited by law, regulation, or an agreement, may continue because the permissible event or actions were established before being prohibited.

Guaranteed Letter of Credit

A letter of credit guaranteed by the customer (applicant) and often backed by collateral security. In domestic banks, the payment of drafts drawn under such a credit is recorded in the general ledger asset account "Customer Liability—Drafts Paid Under Guaranteed L/C."

H

Hedging

Attempt to reduce interest rate risk by investing in shorter-term assets or funding long-term liabilities; also attempts to reduce risk in market fluctuations by contracting equal and opposite positions (futures, options, currency contracts) to an existing transaction.

Highly Leveraged Transaction

Credit extension to, or investment in, a business where the financing transaction involves the buyout, acquisition, or recapitalization of an existing business. Tests for qualifying as an HLT include meeting one of the following:

1. The transaction doubles, at a minimum, the subject company's liabilities and results in a leverage ratio higher than 50 percent;

2. Transaction results in a leverage ratio higher than 75 percent; or

3. Transaction is designated a highly leveraged transaction by a syndication agent. This definition has been jointly defined by the OCC, FDIC, and Federal Reserve.

Holding Company

Parent company; a company that directly or indirectly controls another. *See* Regulation Y 12 CFR 225 for further definition, including detail on term *Bank Holding Company*.

Home Equity Line of Credit

An open-end fixed or variable rate credit plan that is secured by the consumer's dwelling.

Home Improvement Loan

REGULATION C, 12 CFR 203.2 (f)

"Any loan that

(1) is stated by the borrower (at the time of the loan application) to be for the purchase of repairing, rehabilitating, or remodeling a residential dwelling (including a condominium, cooperative, or mobile or manufactured home) located in a state; and

(2) is classified by the financial institution as a home-improvement loan."

Home Purchase Loan

REGULATION C, 12 CFR 203.2 (g)

"Any loan secured by and made for the purpose of purchasing, or refinancing the purchase of, a residential dwelling (including a condominium, cooperative, or mobile or manufactured home) located in a state."

Hypothecated Deposit

The aggregation of periodic payments on an installment contract received by an institution in a state in which, under law, such payments are not immediately used to reduce the unpaid balance of the installment note but are accumulated until the sum of the payments equals the entire amount of principal and interest on the contract, at which time the loan is considered paid in full.

I

Immediate Family

REGULATION O, 12 CFR 215.2 (e)

"The spouse of an individual, the individual's minor children, and any of the individual's children (including adults) residing in the individual's home."

Inadvertent Error

REGULATION B, 12 CFR 202.2 (s)

"A mechanical, electronic, or clerical error that a creditor demonstrates was not intentional and occurred notwithstanding the maintenance of procedures reasonably adapted to avoid such errors."

Indirectly Secured

REGULATION U, 12 CFR 221.2 (g)

"Includes any arrangement with the customer under which:

(1) the customer's right or ability to sell, pledge, or otherwise dispose of margin stock owned by the customer is in any way restricted while the credit remains outstanding; or

(2) the exercise of such right is or may be cause for accelerating the maturity of the credit.

'Indirectly secured' does not include such an arrangement if

1. after applying the proceeds of the credit, not more than 25 percent of the value (as determined by any reasonable method) of the assets subject to the arrangement is represented by margin stock;

2. it is a lending arrangement that permits accelerating the maturity of the credit as a result of a default or renegotiation of another credit to the customer by another lender that is not an affiliate of the bank;

3. the bank holds the margin stock only in the capacity of custodian, depositary, or trustee, or under similar circumstances, and, in good faith, has not relied upon the margin stock as collateral; or

4. the bank, in good faith, has not relied upon the margin stock as collateral in extending or maintaining the particular credit."

Insider

Person, serving as an officer, director, or principal owner, who may have special knowledge or access to confidential information of an organization or financial institution.

Inspection Report

Progress report on construction activities, completed by an objective professional not associated with the borrower or contractor. Report details project, estimated completion to date,and estimated value that in general correlates to the amount advanced by the financial institution for the construction project.

Name of examination report used by certain regulatory agencies.

Interest

REGULATION Q, 12 CFR 217.2 (d)

"Any payment to or for the account of any depositor as compensation for the use of funds constituting a deposit. A member bank's absorption of expenses incident to providing a normal banking function or its forbearance from charging a fee in connection with such a service is not considered a payment of interest."

Interest Arbitrage

Involves the movement of short-term funds from one currency to another for the purpose of investing idle funds at a higher yield. However, the real yield advantage in such a situation is not merely the difference in interest rates between the two investment choices but, rather, is the subtraction of the cost of transferring funds into the desired currency and back again from the interest differential. There are four types of interest arbitrage:

1. Covered interest arbitrage—transfer of short-term funds into a foreign currency for the sake of a higher yield, with the exchange risk covered;

2. Inward interest arbitrage—transfer of short-term funds into local currency for a higher yield;

3. Outward interest arbitrage—transfer of short-term funds into a foreign currency for a higher yield; and

4. Uncovered interest arbitrage—transfer of short-term funds into a foreign currency for a higher yield, without covering the exchange risk.

Interest Rate Risk

Sensitivity of net asset values and earnings to changes in interest rates. Risk to a bank's earnings arise from a bank's accrual business and from its positions carried on a market valuation basis and risk to the market value of portfolio equity arising from a bank's long-term fixed rate positions.

Internal Rate of Return

Rate of return of investment in an asset. For example, internal rate of return would be calculated by finding the discount rate that equates the present discount value of future cash flows to the cost of the investment such as capital dollars invested.

International Banking Facility (IBF)

A set of asset and liability accounts, segregated on the books and records of the establishing entity, which reflects international transactions. An IBF is established in accordance with the terms of Federal Reserve Regulation D and after appropriate notification to the Federal Reserve. The establishing entity may be a U.S. office of an Edge or agreement corporation, or a U.S. branch or agency of a foreign bank pursuant to Federal Reserve Regulations D and Q. An IBF is permitted to hold only certain assets and liabilities. In general, IBF accounts are limited to non-U.S. residents of foreign countries, residents of Puerto Rico and U.S. territories and possessions, other IBFs, and U.S. and non-U.S. offices of the establishing entity.

International Monetary Fund (IMF)

A specialized agency of the United Nations. It encourages monetary cooperation, establishes international standards for exchange policy, promotes stable exchange policy, promotes stable exchange rates among 114 member nations, and makes short-term advances and standby credits to members experiencing temporary payments difficulties. Its resources come mainly from subscriptions of members.

International Organization

REGULATION J, 12 CFR 210.2 (l) (3)

"An international organization is one for which a Reserve Bank is empowered to act as depository or fiscal agent and maintains an account."

Interoffice Transaction

REGULATION J, 12 CFR 210.26 (b)

"A transfer between a transferor and transferee that do not maintain or use accounts at the same office of a Reserve Bank."

Investment

REGULATION K, 12 CFR 211.2 (i)

"The ownership or control of shares (including partnership interests and other interests evidencing ownership), binding commitments to acquire shares, contributions to the capital and surplus of an organization, and the holding of an organization's subordinated debt when shares of the organization are also held by the investor or the investor's affiliate."

Investment Banker

Brokerage firm, securities dealer or other brokering organization that assists lenders in selling or buying loans or raising funds in the capital market.

Investor

REGULATION K, 12 CFR 211.2 (j)

"An Edge corporation, agreement corporation, bank holding company, or member bank."

Item

REGULATION J, 12 CFR 210.2 (g)

"An instrument for the payment of money, whether negotiable or not, that is

(1) payable in a Federal Reserve District (*See* Regulation J for a clarification of 'district');

(2) sent by a sender to a Reserve Bank for handling under Subpart A of Regulation J; and

(3) collectible in funds acceptable to the Reserve Bank of the district in which the instrument is payable.

Unless otherwise indicated, 'item' includes both cash and noncash items. 'Item' does not include a check that cannot be collected at par, or an 'item' as defined in section 210.26 that is handled under Subpart B. Unless otherwise indicated, 'item' includes both a cash and a noncash item, and includes a returned check sent by a paying or returning bank. 'Item' does not include a check that cannot be collected at par, or an 'item' as defined in Section 210.26 that is handled under Subpart B."

REGULATION J, 12 CFR 210.26 (c)

"A writing evidencing a request for the payment of money, that is handled under Subpart B of Regulation J. 'Item' does not include an 'item' as defined inSection 210.2 that is handled under Subpart A of Regulation J."

J

Joint Venture

REGULATION K, 12 CFR 211.2 (k)

"An organization that has 20 percent or more of its voting shares held directly or indirectly by the investor or by an affiliate of the investor, but which is not a subsidiary of the investor."

Judgmental System of Evaluating Applicants

REGULATION B, 12 CFR 202.2 (t)

"Any system for evaluating the creditworthiness of an applicant other than an empirically derived, demonstrably and statistically sound, credit scoring system."

L

Lead Lender

Financial institution that originates a large line of credit and then sells participations to other financial institutions.

Lease

A contract whereby one party, known as the lessor, grants to another party, known as the lessee, the rights of use, tenancy, or occupancy to property owned by the lessor. This property may be land, buildings, equipment, or other chattel property. The lease agreement describes the rights of the owner (lessor) and the renter (lessee), and recites the terms of periodic payment and the tenure of the lease. Types of leases include capital lease (a sale financing arrangement or sometimes called a financing lease), full payout lease, general lease, leveraged lease, net lease, operating lease, and service lease.

Lease of Personal Property

REGULATION M, 12 CFR 213.2 (a) (4)

"To provide or offer to provide a lease which is or will be extended by another person under a business or other relationship pursuant to which the person arranging such lease:

(i) receives or will receive a fee, compensation, or other consideration for such service; or

(ii) has knowledge of the lease terms and participates in the preparation of the contract documents required in connection with the lease."

Lender

THE DEPARTMENT OF HOUSING AND URBAN DEVELOPMENT'S REGULATION X, 24 CFR 3500.2 (c)

"The secured creditor or creditors named as such in the debt obligation and document creating the lien or other security interest."

Lending Limit

REGULATION O, 12 CFR 215.2 (f)

"For a member bank is an amount equal to the limit on loans to a single borrower established by Section 5200 of the Revised Statutes, 12 USC 84. This amount is 15 percent of the bank's unimpaired capital and unimpaired surplus in the case of loans that are not fully secured, and an additional 10 percent of the bank's unimpaired capital and unimpaired surplus in the case of loans that are fully secured by readily marketable collateral having a market value, as determined by reliable and continuously available price quotations, at least equal to the amount of the loan. The lending limit also includes any higher amounts that are permitted by Section 5200 of the Revised Statutes for the types of obligations listed therein as exceptions to the limit. A member bank's capital stock and unimpaired surplus equals the sum of

(1) the 'total equity capital' of the member bank reported on its most recent consolidated report of condition filed under 12 USC 1817(a)(3),

(2) any subordinated notes and debentures approved as an addition to the member bank's capital structure by the appropriate federal banking agency, and

(3) any valuation reserves created by charges to the member bank's income."

Lessee

REGULATION M, 12 CFR 213.2 (a) (7)

"A natural person who leases under, or who is offered a consumer lease."

Lessor

REGULATION M, 12 CFR 213.2 (a) (8)

"A person who, in the ordinary course of business regularly leases, offers to lease, or arranges for the leasing of personal property under a consumer lease."

Letter of Credit (LC)

A document issued by a bank on behalf of its customer (the account party) authorizing a third party (the beneficiary) or, in special cases the account party, to draw drafts on the bank up to a stipulated amount and with specified terms and conditions. The letter of credit is a conditional commitment (except when prepaid by the account party) on the part of the bank to provide payment on drafts drawn in accordance with the terms of the document. Types of letters of credit include back-to-back commercial letter of credit, documentary letter of credit, clean letter of credit, commercial letter of credit, guaranteed letter of credit, paid letter of credit, revocable letter of credit, sight letter of credit, standby letter of credit, straight letter of credit, time or accept letter of credit, traveler's letter of credit, and various types of irrevocable letters of credit. *See* also **Advised Letter of Credit.**

Letter of Credit Sold for Cash

A letter of credit for which the bank has received funds from the account party at the time of issuance. These letters are considered to have been sold for cash even though the bank may have advanced funds to the account party for the purchase of such letters of credit on a secured or unsecured basis.

Leveraged Buyout (LBO)

See **Highly Leveraged Transaction.**

Leverage Ratio

Total liabilities divided by total assets.

Lien

Claim that a lender has against property owned by a customer, serving as security for the repayment of debt.

Limited Life Preferred Stock

A preferred stock that has a maturity date or that can be redeemed at the option of the holder. It excludes those issues of preferred stock that automatically convert into perpetual preferred stock or common stock at a stated date.

Line of Credit

Agreement between financial institution and borrower regarding amount of funds that it will grant the customer over a future time frame. The customer does not pay a commitment fee to have the line available and will pay interest only on the amount borrowed.

Liquidity

Ability to convert assets into cash without incurring a loss; the management of a financial institution tries to balance liquidity needs against income objectives.

Listed Securities

Securities such as stocks and bonds that are recognized and carried on a known stock exchange organization and available for trading on that exchange.

Loan

A loan is generally an extension of credit resulting from direct negotiations between a lender and a borrower. A bank may originate a loan by directly negotiating with a borrower or it may purchase a loan or a portion of a loan originated by another lender that directly negotiated with a borrower. A bank may also sell a loan or a portion of a loan, regardless of the method by which it acquired the loan.

Loans may take the form of promissory notes, acknowledgements of advance, due bills, invoices, overdrafts, commercial paper, acceptances, and similar written or oral obligations.

Loan Commitment

Binding legal obligation to advance money per stated terms, conditions, etc. Lenders often charge a fee for such commitments.

Loan Participation

Buying portions of outstanding loan balances by purchasers, the buyers participate on a *pro rata* basis in collecting interest and principal payments. Loss in terms of uncollectible interest and principal may or may not be shared equally depending on the terms of the underlying loan participation agreement.

Loan Review

Reviews conducted to determine the ultimate collectability of a financial institution's loan portfolio. Loan review focuses include measuring compliance with internal loan policies, providing objective appraisals to management and the board of directors regarding the impact on the bank, regarding current and potential loan problems, and establishing an early warning identification system for problem loans.

Local Check

REGULATION CC, 12 CFR 229.2 (r)

"A check payable by or at a local paying bank, or a check payable by a nonbank payor and payable through a local paying bank."

Local Paying Bank

REGULATION CC, 12 CFR 229.2 (s)

"A paying bank that is located in the same check-processing region as the physical location of:

(1) the branch or proprietary ATM of the depository bank in which that check was deposited; or

(2) both the branch of the depositary bank at which the account is held and the nonproprietary ATM at which the check is deposited."

London Interbank Offered Rate (LIBOR)

An acronym standing for the London Interbank Offered Rate. This is the rate at which, theoretically, banks in London place Eurocurrencies/Eurodollars with each other.

Loss Classification

Designation assigned to assets that are deemed uncollectible and of minimal value, such that their notation as assets without establishment of a loan loss reserve specifically reserving for those assets is unwarranted. The classification does not mean that the asset has absolutely no recovery opportunity or salvage value but indicates that the asset is no longer suitable for unreserved balance sheet presentation.

Low Quality Asset

THE FEDERAL RESERVE ACT SECTION 23A (b) (10)

"An asset that falls in any one or more of the following categories:

(A) an asset classified as 'substandard,' 'doubtful,' or 'loss' or treated as 'other loans especially mentioned' in the most recent report of examination or inspection of an affiliate prepared by either a federal or state supervisory agency;

(B) an asset in a nonaccrual status;

(C) an asset on which principal or interest payments are more than thirty days past due; or

(D) an asset whose terms have been renegotiated or compromised due to the deteriorating financial condition of the obligor."

M

Majority Owned Subsidiary

A majority owned subsidiary of a bank is a subsidiary in which the parent bank directly or indirectly owns more than 50 percent of the outstanding voting stock of the subsidiary.

Management Official

REGULATION L, 212.2 (h)

(1)(i) "An employee or officer with management functions (including a branch manager);

(ii) a director (including an advisory director or honorary director);

(iii) a trustee of a business organization under the control of trustees (e.g., a mutual savings bank); or

(iv) any person who has a representative or nominee serving in any such capacity."

(2) Management official does not include

(i) a person whose management functions relate exclusively to the business of retail merchandising or manufacturing;

(ii) a person whose management functions relate principally to the business outside the United States of a foreign commercial bank; or

(iii) persons described in the provisos of Section 202(4) of the Interlocks Act (12 USC 3201[4])."

Mandatorily Convertible Securities

There are two types of mandatorily convertible securities;

1. Equity contract notes, which require the holder to take common or perpetual preferred stock of the issuer in lieu of cash for repayment of principal; and

2. Equity commitment notes securities, which are redeemable only with the proceeds from the sale of common or preferred perpetual stock.

Margin Stock

REGULATION U, 12 CFR 221.2 (h)

(1) "Any equity security registered or having unlisted trading privileges on a national securities exchange;

(2) Any OTC margin stock;

(3) Any OTC security designated as qualified for trading in the National Market System under a designation plan approved by the Securities and Exchange Commission (NMS security);

(4) Any debt security issued by an investment company registered under Section 8 of the Investment Company Act of 1940 (15 USC 80a-8), other than

(i) a company licensed under the Small Business Investment Act of 1958, as amended (15 USC 661); or

(ii) a company which has at least 95 percent of its assets continuously invested in exempted securities (as defined in 15 USC 78c[a]([12]); or

(iii) a company which issues face-amount certificates as defined in 15 USC 80a-2(a)(15), but only with respect of such securities."

Marital Status

REGULATION B, 12 CFR 202.2 (u)

"The state of being unmarried, married, or separated, as defined by applicable state law. The term 'unmarried' includes persons who are single, divorced, or widowed."

Market Value

The highest price estimated in terms of money, which a buyer would be warranted in paying and a seller justified in accepting, provided both parties were fully informed, acted intelligently and voluntarily, and that all the rights and benefits inherent in, or attributable to, the property were included in the transfer. At any given moment of time, market value connotes what a property is actually worth and what it can be sold for. The amounts may or may not coincide, since current supply and demand factors enter strongly into market price.

Maturity Gap

Mismatched asset and liability maturities creating days or periods of uneven cash inflows and outflows. A substantial inflow of a particular currency over a prolonged period may result in excess idle funds for which no investment or sale has been arranged. This could mean a loss of income on the idle funds for that period and/or of the amount by which the value of that currency is expected to appreciate or depreciate. Conversely, substantial outflows prior to the maturities of offsetting assets may necessitate purchasing or borrowing the required currency for that period (gap) at substantial higher rates. Thus, the bank is exposed to the risk of rate changes between the time the gap was created and the date it is actually closed.

Maximum Loan Value

REGULATION U, 12 CFR 221.2 (i)

"The percentage of current market value assigned by the Federal Reserve Board under Section 221.8 of Regulation U to specified types of collateral. The maximum loan value of margin stock is stated as a percentage of its current market value. Puts, calls, and combinations thereof have no loan value except for purposes of Section 221.5 (c) (10) of Regulation U. All other collateral has good faith loan value."

Member Bank

REGULATION O, 12 CFR 215.2 (g)

"Any banking institution that is a member of the Federal Reserve System. The term does not include any foreign bank (as defined in 12 USC 3101[7]) that maintains a branch in the United States, whether or not the branch is insured (within the meaning of 12 USC 1813[s]) and regardless of the operation of 12 USC 1813(h) and 12 USC 1828(j)(2)."

Merger

The combining of the assets, liabilities, and capital accounts of two banks with the target bank ceasing to exist. The target bank is dissolved and its charter is returned to the chartering regulatory agency. The target bank's shareholders have dissenters' rights.

Merger Transaction

REGULATION CC, 12 CFR 229.2 (t)

(1) "A merger or consolidation of two or more banks; or

(2) The transfer of substantially all of the assets of one or more banks or branches to another bank in consideration of the assumption by the acquiring bank of substantially all of the liabilities of the transferring banks, including the deposit liabilities."

Metropolitan Statistical Area (MSA)

REGULATION C, 12 CFR 203.2 (h)

"A metropolitan statistical area or a primary metropolitan statistical area is a specific geographical area that is defined by the U.S. Office of Management and Budget."

Mortgage-backed Pass-through Securities

Securities that convey ownership of a fractional part of each mortgage in a pool of mortgages backing that security.

Mortgaged Property

PER THE DEPARTMENT OF HOUSING AND URBAN DEVELOPMENT'S REGULATION X, 24 CFR 3500.2 (d)

The real property covered by the "federally related mortgage loan" (defined under Section 3500.5 [b]), or the cooperative unit with respect to which stock is pledged to secure the federally related mortgage loan.

Municipal Securities Rulemaking Board (MSRB)

Created in 1975 under the Securities Act Amendments, MSRB is a self-regulatory organization that represents firms operating in the securities markets and is responsible for the enforcement of fair, efficient, and ethical practices in the securities industry. MSRB regulates all dealers, brokers, and banks dealing in municipal securities. MSRB makes rules, which are reviewed and approved by the SEC and enforced by bank regulatory agencies and NASD.

Mutual Savings Bank

REGULATION H, 12 CFR 208.1 (b)

"A bank without capital stock transacting a savings bank business, the net earnings of which inure wholly to the benefit of its depositors after payment of obligations for any advances by its organizers, and in addition thereto includes any other banking institution, the capital of which consists of weekly or other time deposits which are segregated from all other deposits and are regarded as capital stock for the purposes of taxation and the declaration of dividends."

N

Natural Person

REGULATION D, 12 CFR 204.2 (g)

"An individual or a sole proprietorship. The term does not mean a corporation owned by an individual, a partnership, or other association."

Negative Amortization

Repayment schedule calling for periodic payments that are insufficient to fully amortize the loan. Earned, but unpaid interest is added to the principal, increasing the debt. Eventually, payments must be rescheduled to fully pay off the debt.

Negative Factor or Negative Value

REGULATION B, 12 CFR 202.2 (v)

"In relation to the age of elderly applicants, means utilizing a factor, value, or weight that is less favorable regarding elderly applicants than the creditor's experience warrants or is less favorable than the factor, value, or weight assigned to the class of applicants that are not classified as elderly and are most favored by a creditor on the basis of age."

Negotiable Order of Withdrawal (NOW) Account

An interest-earning account on which checks may be drawn. Withdrawals from NOW accounts may be subject to a fourteen-day or more notice requirement although such is rarely imposed. NOW accounts may be offered by commercial banks, mutual savings banks, and savings and loan associations, and may be owned only by individuals and certain nonprofit organizations and governmental units.

Net Interest Income

Difference between total interest income and total interest expense.

Net Transaction Accounts

REGULATION D, 12 CFR 204.2 (j)

"The total amount of a depository institution's transaction accounts less the deductions allowed under the provisions of Section 204.3 of Regulation D."

Nonbank Payor

REGULATION J, 12 CFR 210.2 (h)

"A payor of an item, other than a bank."

Nonbank Servicer

An EDP (electronic data processing) servicer that is not a department or subsidiary of a bank.

Noncash Item

REGULATION J, 12 CFR 210.2 (i)

"An item that a receiving Federal Reserve Bank classifies in its operating circulars as requiring special handling. The term also means an item normally received as a cash item if a Federal Reserve Bank decides that special conditions require that it handle the item as a noncash item."

REGULATION CC, 12 CFR 229.2 (u)

"An item that would otherwise be a check, except that:

(1) a passbook, certificate, or other document is attached;

(2) it is accompanied by special instructions, such as a request for special advice of payment or dishonor;

(3) it consists of more than a single thickness of paper, except a check that qualifies for handling by automated check-processing equipment; or

(4) it has not been preprinted or post-encoded in magnetic ink with the routing number of the paying bank."

Nonlocal Check

REGULATION CC, 12 CFR 229.2 (v)

"A check payable by, through, or at a nonlocal paying bank."

Nonlocal Paying Bank

REGULATION CC, 12 CFR 229.2 (w)

"A paying bank that is not a local paying bank with respect to the depository bank."

Nonpersonal Time Deposit

REGULATION D, 12 CFR 204.2 (f)

(1)(i) "A time deposit, including a 'money market deposit account' (MMDA) or any other savings deposit, representing funds in which any beneficial interest is held by a depositor which is not a natural person;

(ii) A time deposit, including a MMDA or any other savings deposit, that represents funds deposited to the credit of a depositor that is not a natural person, other than a deposit to the credit of a trustee or other fiduciary if the entire beneficial interest in the deposit is held by one or more natural persons;

(iii) A time deposit that is transferable, except a time deposit originally issued before October 1, 1980, to and held by one or more natural persons, including a deposit to the credit of a trustee or other fiduciary if the entire beneficial interest in the deposit is held by one or more natural persons;

(iv) A time deposit that is transferable, issued on or after October 1, 1980, to and held by one or more natural persons, including a deposit to the credit of a trustee or other fiduciary if the entire beneficial interest is held by one or more natural persons. A time deposit is transferable unless it contains a specific statement on the certificate, instrument, passbook, statement, or other form representing the account that it is not transferable. A time deposit that contains a specific statement that it is not transferable is not regarded as transferable even if the following transactions can be effected: a pledge as collateral for a loan; a transaction that occurs due to circumstances arising from death, incompetency, marriage, divorce, attachment, or otherwise by operation of law or transfer on the books or records of the institution; and

(v) A time deposit represented by a promissory note, an acknowledgement of advance, or similar obligation described in Section 204.2(a)(1)(vii) that is issued to, or any banker's acceptance (other than the type described in 12 USC 372) of the depository institution held by:

(A) any office located outside the United States of another depository institution or Edge or agreement corporation organized under the laws of the United States,

(B) any office located outside the United States of a foreign bank,

(C) a foreign national government, or an agency or instrumentality thereof, engaged principally in activities which are ordinarily performed in the United States by government entities,

(D) an international entity of which the United States is a member, or

(E) any other foreign, international, or supranational entity specifically designated by the Federal Reserve Board.

(2) 'Nonpersonal Time Deposit' does not include nontransferable time deposits to the credit of or in which the entire beneficial interest is held by an individual pursuant to an individual retirement account or Keogh (H.R.10) plan under 26 USC (IRC 1954) 408,401, or nontransferable time deposits held by an employer as part of an unfunded deferred-compensation plan established pursuant to Subtitle D of the Revenue Act of 1978 (Pub. L No. 95-600, 92 Stat. 2763).

(3) Any nonpersonal time deposit with a stated maturity or notice period of one and one-half years or more that permits any early withdrawal must be subject to a minimum early withdrawal penalty equal to at least thirty days' simple interest on the amount withdrawn for any withdrawal that occurs more than six days but within one and one-half years after the date of deposit. Any such account not subject to this minimum early withdrawal penalty will be regarded as a nonpersonal time deposit with an original maturity or notice period of from seven days to less than one and one-half years from the date of the deposit."

Nonproprietary ATM

REGULATION CC, 12 CFR 229.2 (x)

"An ATM (automatic teller machine) that is not a proprietary ATM. Nonproprietary ATMs are ATMs which are available for use by customers to access other financial institutions on a transaction fee basis." *See* PROPRIETARY ATM.

Nonrecourse

Credit provision that relieves the seller from any liability for nonpayment by the obligor.

Nostro Accounts

Demand accounts of banks with their correspondents in foreign countries, which are in the latter's currencies. Such accounts are used to make and receive payments in foreign currencies for a bank's customers and to settle maturing foreign exchange contracts. Also called "due from foreign bank—demand accounts," "our balances with them," or "due from balances."

Notional Amount

Stated dollar amount of an agreement on which interest rate payments are determined for interest rate contracts, that is, swaps, caps.

O

Office

REGULATION L, 12 CFR 212.2 (i)

"A principal or branch office, located in the United States, of a depository institution. 'Office' does not include a representative office of a foreign commercial bank, an electronic terminal, a loan production office, or any office of a depository holding company."

Offset

Closing out one position by entering into another position opposite the originally established one.

Open-end Credit

REGULATION B, 12 CFR 202.2 (w)

"Credit extended under a plan wherein a creditor may permit an applicant to make purchases or obtain loans from time to time directly from the creditor or indirectly by use of a credit card, check, or other device."

REGULATION Z, 12 CFR 226.2 (a) (20)

"Consumer credit extended by a creditor under a plan in which:

(i) the creditor reasonably contemplates repeated transactions;

(ii) the creditor may impose a finance charge from time to time on an outstanding unpaid balance; and

(iii) the amount of credit that may be extended to the consumer during the term of the plan (up to any limit set by the creditor) is generally made available to the extent that any outstanding balance is repaid."

Operating Subsidiary

Corporation in which the majority of stock is owned by an insured financial institution. The activities of the operating subsidiary are part of or incidental to the business of the institution, as authorized by law governing the institution.

Option

A right to buy (call) or sell (put) a fixed amount of a given stock at a specified price within a limited period of time. The purchaser hopes that the stock's price will go up (if he bought a call) or down (if he bought a put) by an amount sufficient to provide a profit greater than the cost of the contract and the commission, and other fees required to exercise the contract.

Order Bill of Lading

A bill of lading drawn to the order of a certain party, usually the shipper or a bank, whose endorsement is required to effect negotiability. The title then passes to the holder.

Organization

REGULATION K, 12 CFR 211.2 (l)

"A corporation, government, partnership, association, or any other entity."

REGULATION M, 12 CFR 213.2 (a) (9)

"A corporation, trust, estate, partnership, cooperative, association, government, or governmental subdivision, agency, or instrumentality."

Organizational Costs

Costs incurred in the formation of an institution such as the legal, accounting, consulting, and/or secretarial costs related to the application for a charter, preparation of articles of association and bylaws, and costs of selling stock and obtaining insurance.

Other Loans Especially Mentioned (Other Assets Especially Mentioned)

Criticized category denoting assets that currently are protected but are potentially weak. Accordingly, such assets constitute an undue and unwarranted credit risk but at present do not warrant a more severe rating.

Other Real Estate Owned

See REAL ESTATE OWNED.

Over the Counter (OTC) Margin Stock

REGULATION U, 12 CFR 221.2 (j)

"Any equity security not traded on a national security exchange that the Board of Governors of the Federal Reserve System has determined has the degree of national investor interest, the depth and breadth of market, the availability of information respecting the security and the issuer, and the character and permanence of the issuer to warrant being treated like an equity security traded on a national securities exchange. An OTC stock is not considered to be an 'OTC margin stock' unless it appears on the Board's periodically published list of OTC margin stocks."

Overdraft (OD)

An overdraft can be either planned or unplanned. An unplanned overdraft occurs when a depository institution honors a check or draft drawn against a deposit account when insufficient funds are on deposit and there is no advance contractual agreement to honor the check or draft. When a contractual agreement has been made in advance to allow such credit extensions, overdrafts are referred to as planned or prearranged. Any overdraft, whether planned or unplanned, is an extension of credit.

P

Par Value

When applied to common stock, it refers to an arbitrary dollar amount assigned to each share by the company's charter. The amount has little significance to the actual market value. In the case of preferred stock and bonds, par value is important, however, as the preferred dividend or interest on the bond is often based on par value assigned to each issue. An 8 percent bond is a promise to pay that percentage of the bond's par (100 percent of face value) value annually. Also, it is the amount to be received in cash at maturity of a bond.

Participant

REGULATION CC, 12 CFR 229.2 (y)

"A bank that:

(1) is located in the geographical area served by a check clearinghouse association; and

(2) both collects and receives for payment checks through the check clearinghouse association either directly or through another participant."

Pass-through Account

REGULATION D, 12 CFR 204.2 (l)

"A balance maintained by a depository institution that is not a member bank, by a U.S. branch or agency of a foreign bank, or by an Edge or agreement corporation:

(1) in an institution that maintains required reserve balances at a Federal Reserve Bank,

(2) in a Federal Home Loan Bank,

(3) in the National Credit Union Administration Central Liquidity Facility, or

(4) in an institution that has been authorized by the Board to pass through required reserve balances if the institution, Federal Home Loan Bank, or National Credit Union Administration Central Liquidity Facility maintains the funds in the form of a balance in a Federal Reserve Bank of which it is a member or at which it maintains an account in accordance with rules and regulations of the Board of Governors of the Federal Reserve System."

Pass-through Reserve Balances

Under the Monetary Control Act of 1980 and as reflected in Federal Reserve Regulation D, depository institutions that are members of the Federal Reserve System must maintain their required reserves (in excess of vault cash) directly with a Federal Reserve Bank. However, nonmember depository institutions may maintain their required reserves (in excess of vault cash) in one of two ways: either

(1) directly with a Federal Reserve Bank or

(2) indirectly in an account with another institution (referred to here as a "correspondent"), which, in turn, is required to pass the reserves through to a Federal Reserve Bank. This second type of account is called a "pass-through account," and a depository institution passing its reserves to the Federal Reserve through a correspondent is referred to here as a "respondent."

Password

A unique word or string of characters that a program, computer operator, or user must supply to meet security requirements, before gaining access to data.

Patching

An area of computer compliance safety and soundness evaluations. Patching represents the correcting or modifying of a program in a rough or expedient way by adding new sections of coding. Patches should be used only as temporary modifications of object language, as opposed to a change in the source program.

Pay an Overdraft on an Account

REGULATION O, 12 CFR 215.2 (h)

"To pay an amount upon the order of an account holder in excess of funds on deposit in the account."

Paying Bank

REGULATION CC, 12 CFR 229.2 (z)

(1) "The bank by which a check is payable, unless the check is payable at another bank and is sent to the other bank for payment and collection;

(2) The bank at or through which a check is payable and to which it is sent for payment or collection;

(3) The Federal Reserve Bank or Federal Home Loan Bank by which a check is payable;

(4) The bank through which a check is payable and to which it is sent for payment or collection, if the check is not payable by a bank; or

(5) The state or unit of general local government on which a check is drawn and to which it is sent for payment or collection. For purposes of Subpart C of Regulation CC, and in connection therewith, Subpart A, 'paying bank' includes the bank through which a check is payable and to which the check is sent for payment or collection, regardless of whether the check is payable by another bank, and the bank whose routing number appears on a check in fractional or magnetic form and to which the check is sent for payment or collection."

REGULATION J, 12 CFR 210.2 (j)

(1) "The bank by which an item is payable, unless the item

is payable or collectable at or through another bank and is sent to the other bank for payment or collection;

(2) The bank at or through which an item is payable or collectable and to which it is sent for payment or collection; or

(3) The bank whose routing number appears on a check in magnetic characters or fractional form and to which the check is sent for payment or collection."

Peer Group

Group of institutions within a given asset size and/or geographic location. Usually utilized for performance comparisons purposes.

Percentage Interest Margin

The interest margin divided by average earning assets.

Period

REGULATION M, 12 CFR 213.2 (a) (10)

"A day, week, month, or other subdivision of a year."

Periodic Rate

REGULATION Z, 12 CFR 226.2 (a) (21)

"A rate of finance charge that is or may be imposed by a creditor on a balance for a day, week, month, or other subdivision of a year."

Perpetual Preferred Stock

Preferred stock that does not have a stated maturity date or that cannot be redeemed at the option of the holder. It includes those issues of preferred stock that automatically convert into common stock at a stated date.

Person

REGULATION B, 12 CFR 202.2 (x)

"A natural person, corporation, government, or governmental subdivision or agency, trust, estate, partnership, cooperative, or association."

REGULATION K, 12 CFR 211.2 (m)

"An individual or an organization."

REGULATION L, 12 CFR 212.2 (j)

"A natural person, corporation, or other business."

REGULATION M, 12 CFR 213.2 (a) (11)

"A natural person or an organization."

REGULATION O, 12 CFR 215.2 (i)

"An individual or a company."

REGULATION S, 12 CFR 219.2 (d)

"An individual or a partnership of five or fewer individuals."

REGULATION Z, 12 CFR 226.2 (a) (22)

"A natural person or an organization, including a corporation, partnership, proprietorship, association, cooperative, estate, trust, or government unit."

THE DEPARTMENT OF HOUSING AND URBAN DEVELOPMENT'S REGULATION X, 24 CFR 3500.2 (e)

"Any individual, corporation, partnership, trust, association, or other entity."

Personal Guaranty

Legal agreement signed by an individual stating that they will promise to repay a debt in the event the borrower fails to perform.

Personal Property

REGULATION M, 12 CFR 213.2 (a) (12)

"Any property which is not real property under the law of the state where it is located at the time it is offered or made available for lease."

Pertinent Element of Creditworthiness

REGULATION B, 12 CFR 202.2 (y)

"In relation to a judgmental system of evaluating applicants, means any information about applicants that a creditor obtains and considers and that has a demonstrable relationship to a determination of creditworthiness."

Points

Finance charges paid by the borrower at the beginning of a loan in addition to monthly interest; each point equals one percent of the loan amount.

Portfolio Investment

REGULATION K, 12 CFR 211.2 (n)

"An investment in an organization other than a subsidiary or joint venture."

Preauthorized Electronic Fund Transfer

REGULATION E, 12 CFR 205.2 (j)

"An electronic fund transfer authorized in advance to recur at substantially regular intervals."

Preferred Stock

A form of ownership interest in a bank or other company, which entitles its holders to some preference or priority over the owners of common stock, usually with respect to dividends or asset distributions in a liquidation.

Premium

A premium arises when a bank purchases a security, loan, or other asset at a price in excess of its par or face value, typically because the current level of interest rates for such assets is less than its contract or stated rate of interest. The difference between the purchase price and par or face value represents the premium that all banks are required to amortize.

Prepaid Finance Charge

REGULATION Z, 12 CFR 226.2 (a) (23)

"Any finance charge paid separately in cash or by check before or at consummation of a transaction, or withheld from the proceeds of the credit at any time."

Present Value

Value, discounted at the current interest yield of comparable investments, of a payment or schedule of payments due and payable at a specified date sometime in the future.

Primary Capital

When referring to primary capital, regulatory agencies include the following: common stock, perpetual preferred stock, capital surplus, undivided profits, contingency and other capital reserves (excluding accrued dividends on perpetual and limited life preferred stock), net worth certificates, minority interests in consolidated subsidiaries, and the allowance for loan and lease losses minus intangible assets except those representing purchased rights to service mortgage loans. Primary capital, for OCC purposes as an example, includes mandatory convertible debt in an amount not exceeding 20 percent of the above components.

Prime Rate

The minimum interest rate on bank loans established by large commercial banks and granted to only top business borrowers. The rate is influenced by the type of loan, by general business conditions, the bank's need for loans, interest rates for other investment opportunities, availability of reserves, etc.

Principal Shareholder

REGULATION O, 12 CFR 215.2 (j)

"An individual or a company (other than an insured bank) that directly or indirectly, or acting through or in concert with one or more persons, owns, controls, or has the power to vote more than 10 percent of any class of voting securities of a member bank or company. However, for the purposes of Section 215.4 (c) of Regulation O, this percentage shall be 'more than 18 percent' if the member bank is located in a city, town, or village with a population of less than 30,000. Shares owned or controlled by a member of an individual's immediate family are considered to be held by the individual. A principal shareholder of a member bank includes

(1) a principal shareholder of a bank holding company (as defined in 12 USC 1841[a]) of which the member bank is a subsidiary and

(2) a principal shareholder of any other subsidiary of that bank holding company."

Private Network Sender Net Debit Cap

Network establishes maximum ceiling based on the aggregate net debit position that an individual sender can incur on a single private network at any point in time during the day.

Profit Margin

Net income divided by operating income.

Prohibited Basis

REGULATION B, 12 CFR 202.2 (z)

"Race, color, religion, national origin, sex, marital status, or age (provided that the applicant has the capacity to enter into a binding contract); the fact that all or a part of the applicant's income derives from any public assistance program; or the fact that the applicant has in good faith exercised any right under the Consumer Credit Protection Act or any state law upon which an exemption has been granted by the Board of Governors of the Federal Reserve System."

Proprietary ATM

REGULATION CC, 12 CFR 229.2 (aa)

"An ATM that is:

(1) owned or operated by or operated exclusively for, the depositary bank;

(2) located on the premises (including the outside wall) of the depositary bank; or

(3) located within fifty feet of the premises of the depositary bank, and not identified as being owned or operated by another entity. If more than one bank meets the owned-or-operated criterion of paragraph (1) of this definition, the ATM is considered proprietary to the bank that operates it."

Purchase and Assumption

A bank's acquisition of assets and assumption of liabilities of another bank. This type of acquisition differs from a loan participation or securities purchase in that insured deposits must be acquired (assumed) for the transaction to qualify as a purchase and assumption. The approval of the shareholders of the selling bank is not required.

Purpose Credit

REGULATION U, 12 CFR 221.2 (k)

"Any credit for the purpose, whether immediate, incidental, or ultimate, of buying or carrying margin stock."

Put Option

An optional, delivery forward placement contract. It obligates the seller of the contract to purchase some financial instrument at the option of the buyer of the contract.

Q

Qualified Returned Check

REGULATION CC, 12 CFR 229.2 (bb)

"A returned check that is prepared for automated return to the depositary bank by placing the check in a carrier envelope or placing a strip on the check and encoding the strip or envelope in magnetic ink. A qualified returned check need not contain other elements of a check drawn on the depositary bank, such as the name of the depositary bank."

Qualified Subordinated Debt

Subordinated debt, as defined by various capital regulations, which meets specific requirements in order to be considered in meeting minimum capital requirements.

R

Real Estate Investment Trust (REIT)

An organization similar to an investment company in some respects but concentrating its holdings in real estate investments. The yield generally is liberal since REITs are required to distribute as much as 90 percent of their income.

Real Estate Owned (REO)

Real estate acquired by a financial institution through foreclosure to satisfy debts previously contracted; it may also include property previously obtained in anticipation of future premises expansion but for which such plans no longer exist. Time limits exist for how long property may be held in REO. Also identified as other real estate owned, or OREO.

Real Estate Settlement Procedures Act (RESPA)

RESPA should effect a more effective advance disclosure of settlement costs to home buyers and sellers. Through this process kickbacks or referral fees that historically may have been hidden and/or buried, which resulted in not required fees added to the mortgage fees as part of the closing, are eliminated. Furthermore, RESPA reduced the amounts home buters would be required to place in escrow accounts to insure the payment of real estate taxes and insurance.

Real Property

REGULATION M, 12 CFR 213.2 (a) (13)

"Property which is real property under the law of the state in which it is located. Real property consists of fixed, permanent, immovable elements such as land."

Realized Value

REGULATION M, 12 CFR 213.2 (a) (14)

(i) "The price received by the lessor for the leased property at disposition,

(ii) the highest offer for disposition, or

(iii) the fair market value at the end of the lease term."

Reciprocal Balances

Reciprocal balances arise when two depository institutions maintain deposit accounts with each other; that is, when a reporting bank has both a "due to" and a "due from" balance with another depository institution.

Regulatory Capital

The definition detailed by the appropriate supervisory agency for a financial institution, depending on its charter, which details types and purposes of capital and outlines the minimum regulatory requirements.

Reimbursement Letter of Credit

A letter of credit issued by one bank and payable at a second bank that, in turn, draws on a third bank for reimbursement of the second bank's payment to the beneficiary. Those credits are almost always expressed in a currency other than that of the buyer (issuing bank) or the seller, and because of wide acceptability many are settled in the United States through yet another bank as the reimbursing agent. Upon issuance, the correspondent sends the reimbursing bank an authorization to honor drawings presented by the negotiating bank.

Related Interest

REGULATION O, 12 CFR 215.2 (k)

(1) "A company that is controlled by a person or

(2) A political or campaign committee that is controlled by a person or the funds or services of which will benefit a person."

Relevant Metropolitan Statistical Area

REGULATION L, 12 CFR 212.2 (n)

"A primary metropolitan statistical area, a metropolitan statistical area, or a consolidated metropolitan statistical area that is not comprised of designated primary metropolitan statistical areas as defined by the Office of Management and Budget."

Repossession

To take possession of collateral from a customer that is in default of payments per agreed terms for outstanding loan.

Representative Office

REGULATION K, 12 CFR 211.2 (o)

"An office that engages solely in representational and administrative functions such as solicitation of new business for or liaison between the organization's head office and customers in the United States, and does not have authority to make business decisions for the account of the organization represented."

Representative or Nominee

REGULATION L, 12 CFR 212.2 (k)

"A person who serves as a management official and has an express or implied obligation to act on behalf of another person with respect to management responsibilities. Whether a person is a 'representative or nominee' depends upon the facts in individual cases, and the appropriate federal supervisory agency or agencies will determine, after giving the affected persons an opportunity to respond, whether a person is a 'representative or nominee.' Certain relationships, including family, employment, or agency relationships, or the ability and exercise of ability by a shareholder of a depository organization to elect a director may be evidence of such an express or implied obligation by the management official to another person. For the purposes of this definition, 'person' shall include only natural persons."

Repurchase/Resale Agreements

A repurchase agreement is a transaction involving the sale of assets by one party to another, subject to an agreement by the seller to repurchase the assets back at a specified date or under specified circumstances. A resale agreement (also known as a reverse repurchase agreement) is a transaction involving the purchase of assets by one party from another, which is subject to an agreement by the purchaser to resell the assets at a specified date or in specified circumstances.

Residential Mortgage Transaction

PER REGULATION Z, 12 CFR 226.2 (a) (24)

"A transaction in which a mortgage, deed of trust, purchase money security interest arising under an installment sales contract, or equivalent consensual security interest is created or retained in the consumer's principal dwelling to finance the acquisition or initial construction of that dwelling."

Residual

Amount remaining after all principal and interest payments have been paid to holders of a security.

Retained Earnings

Profits that are not paid out in dividends to shareholders but are instead retained in the bank.

Return on Assets (ROA)

Net income divided by total assets.

Return on Equity (ROE)

Return on assets divided by the result of one minus the total liabilities, divided by the total assets. More simply, net income divided by net worth.

Returned Check

REGULATION J, 12 CFR 210.2 (k)

"A cash item or a check as defined in 12 CFR 229.2 (k) returned by a paying bank, including a notice of nonpayment in lieu of a returned check, whether or not a Reserve Bank handled the check for collection."

Returning Bank

REGULATION CC, 12 CFR 229.2 (cc)

"A bank (other than the paying or depositary bank) handling a returned check or notice in lieu of return. A returning bank is also a collecting bank for purposes of UCC Section 4-202(2)."

Revenue Bonds

A state or local bond whose interest and principal payments are met from the revenues produced by the project financed by the bond issue. Revenue bonds are considered less secure than general obligation bonds because they are not supported by the taxing authority of the state or municipality.

Reverse Repurchase Agreement (RRP)

See Repurchase/Resale Agreements.

Reverse Stock Split

Increases the par value per share with a corresponding reduction in the number of shares outstanding, with no change in common stock. For example, for OCC purposes, 12 USC 52 limits par value to a maximum of $100 per share. A majority vote of shareholders is required.

Revolving Line of Credit

A line of credit that has terms permitting successive drawings and payments at the borrower's discretion. The funds available to the borrower are replenished by any payments of principal.

Risk-Based Capital Reporting Requirements

Simplistically, risk-based capital requirements require all banks and bank holding companies to, as of December 31, 1992, maintain a minimum total risk-based capital ratio of 8 percent with half the capital composed of core capital instruments or contributions.

Routing Number

REGULATION CC, 12 CFR 229.2 (dd)

(1) "The number printed on the face of a check in fractional form or in nine-digit form; or

(2) The number in a bank's endorsement in fractional or nine-digit form."

S

Sale/Leaseback

Transaction in which an entity sells an asset in exchange for cash or other consideration to another; the buyer then in turn contracts to lease the asset to the seller for a specified term.

Salvage Value

Value of an asset at the end of a specified time frame.

Savings Deposit

REGULATION D, 12 CFR 204.2 (d)

(1) "A deposit or account with respect to which the depositor is not required by the deposit contract, but may at any time be required by the depository institution to give written notice of an intended withdrawal not less than seven days before withdrawal is made, and that is not payable on a specified date or at the expiration of a specified time after the date of deposit. The term 'savings deposit' includes a regular share account at a credit union and a regular account at a savings and loan association.

(2) The term 'savings deposit' also means:

(i) a deposit or account that otherwise meets the requirements of Section 204.2(d)(1) and from which, under the terms of the account agreement, or by practice of the depository institution, the depositor is permitted or authorized to make no more than three withdrawals per calendar month, or statement cycle (or similar period) of at least four weeks, for the purpose of transferring funds to another account of the depositor at the same institution (including a 'transaction account') or for making payment to a third party by means of a preauthorized or automatic payment transfer, or telephonic (including data transmission) agreement, order, or instruction, provided that no such withdrawals may be by check, draft, or similar order (including a debit card) drawn by the depositor to third persons. A 'preauthorized transfer' includes any arrangement by the depository institution to pay a third party from the account of a depositor upon written or oral instruction (including an order received through an automated clearinghouse [ACH] or any arrangement by a depository institution to pay a third party from the account of the depositor at a predetermined time or on a fixed schedule. Such an account is not a 'transaction account' by virtue of an arrangement that permits transfers for the purpose of repaying loans and associated expenses at the same depository institution (as originator or servicer) or that permits transfers of funds from the account to another account of the same depositor at the same institution or permits withdrawals (payments directly to the depositor) from the account when such transfers or withdrawals are made by mail, messenger, automated teller machine, or in person or when such withdrawals are made by telephone (via check mailed to the depositor) regardless of the number of such transfers or withdrawals.

(ii) a deposit or account, such as an account commonly known as a 'money market deposit account' (MMDA), that otherwise meets the requirements of Section 204.2(d)(1) and from which, under the terms of the deposit contract or by practice of the depository institution, the depositor is permitted or authorized to make no more than six transfers per calendar month or statement cycle (or similar period) of at least four weeks to another account (including a transaction account) of the depositor at the same institution or to a third party by means of a preauthorized or automatic transfer (*See* Section 204.2 [d] [2] [i], or telephonic (including data transmission) agreement, order, or instruction, and no more than three of the six such transfers may be made by check, draft, debit card, or similar order made by the depositor and payable to third parties. Such an account is not a 'transaction account' by virtue of an arrangement that permits transfers for the purpose of repaying loans and associated expenses at the same depository institution (as originator or servicer) or that permits transfers of funds from this account to another account of the same depositor at the same institution or permits withdrawals (payments directly to the depositor) from the account when such transfers or withdrawals are made by mail, messenger, automated teller machine, or in person, or when such withdrawals are made by telephone (via check mailed to the depositor) regardless of the number of such transfers or withdrawals.

(3) A deposit may continue to be classified as a savings deposit even if the depository institution exercises its right to require notice of withdrawal.

(4) 'Savings deposit' does not include funds deposited to the credit of the depository institution's own trust department where the funds involved are utilized to cover checks or drafts. Such funds are 'transaction accounts'."

Secondary Capital

For regulatory purposes, the OCC has deemed secondary capital to include tht total of limited life preferred stock, subordinated notes and debentures, and mandatory convertible debt that is not included in primary capital up to a maximum of 50 percent of the bank's primary capital.

Securities

THE FEDERAL RESERVE ACT, SECTION 23A (b) (9)

"Stocks, bonds, debentures, notes, or other similar obligations."

Securities and Exchange Commission (SEC)

An independent agency of the U.S. government consisting of five members appointed by the president, which administers comprehensive legislation governing the securities industry.

Securitization

The pooling and repackaging of debt obligations, that is, loans such as charge card receivables and mortgages, into securities that are then perhaps sold into the secondary market.

Security Interest and Security

REGULATION M, 12 CFR 213.2 (a) (15)

"Any interest in property which secures payment or performance of an obligation. The terms include, but are not limited to, security interests under the Uniform Commercial Code, real property mortgages, deeds of trust, and other consensual or confessed liens whether or not recorded, mechanic's, materialman's, artisan's, and other similar liens, vendor's liens in both real and personal property, any lien on property arising by operation of law, and any interest in a lease when used to secure payment or performance of an obligation."

REGULATION Z, 12 CFR 226.2 (a) (25)

"An interest in property that secures performance of a consumer credit obligation and that is recognized by state or federal law. It does not include incidental interests such as interests in proceeds, accessions, additions, fixtures, insurance proceeds (whether or not the creditor is loss payee or beneficiary), premium rebates, or interests in after-acquired property. For purposes of disclosure under Sections 226.6 and 226.18 of Regulation Z, the term does not include an interest that arises solely by operation of law. However, for purposes of the right of rescission under Sections 225.15 and 226.23 of Regulation Z, the term does include interests that arise solely by operation of law."

Self-Assessment

Process of evaluating an institution's creditworthiness, controls, policies, and procedures, as well as credit policies and procedures; process required as part of payment systems risk analysis and establishing daylight overdraft caps.

Seller's Points

A lump sum paid by the seller to the buyer's creditor to reduce the cost of the loan to the buyer. This payment is either required by the creditor or volunteered by the seller, usually in a loan to buy real estate. Generally, one point equals one percent of the loan amount.

Sender

REGULATION J, 12 CFR 210.2 (l)

"Any of the following that sends an item to a Federal Reserve Bank for forward collection: a depository institution, a clearing institution, another Reserve Bank, an international organization, a foreign correspondent, or a branch or agency of a foreign bank maintaining reserves under Section 7 of the International Banking Act of 1978 (12 USC 347d, 3105):

(1) 'Depository institution' means a depository institution as defined in section 19(b) of the Federal Reserve Act (12 USC 461[b]).

(2) 'Clearing institution' means

(i) an institution that is not a depository institution, but maintains with a Reserve Bank the balance referred to in the first paragraph of Section 13 of the Federal Reserve Act (12 USC 342); or

(ii) a corporation that maintains an account with a Reserve Bank in conformity with Section 211.4 of Regulation K.

(3) 'International organization' means an international organization for which a Reserve Bank is empowered to act as depository or fiscal agent and maintains an account.

(4) 'Foreign correspondent' means any of the following for which a Reserve Bank maintains an account: a foreign bank or banker, a foreign state as defined in Section 25(b) of the Federal Reserve Act (12 USC 632), or a foreign correspondent or agency referred to in Section 14(e) of that Act (12 USC 358)."

Sender Risk

Risk that a financial institution assumes when it makes an irrevocable payment on behalf of a customer through an extension of credit.

Servicing Rights

Collection of payments from individual borrowers, the follow-up with delinquent borrowers, and the processing of escrow collections and payments. Servicing rights may either be released with sold loans or retained.

Settlement Risk

Risk that networks assume when payments are provisional or when a system participant is unable to settle its net debt position at the appointed time.

Shell Branches

Limited service branches that do not conduct transactions with residents in the country in which they are located other than with other shell branches. Transactions at shell branches are usually initiated and effected by their head office or by other related branches outside the country in which the shell branches are located, with records and supporting documents maintained at the initiating offices. Examples of such locations are the Bahamas and the Cayman Islands.

Short-term Asset

Repayment of the asset is due within one year.

Short-term Liability

Repayment of the liability is due within one year.

Sight Draft

A draft payable upon presentation to the drawee or within a brief period thereafter known as "days of grace."

Significant Subsidiary

A majority-owned subsidiary that meets any one or more of the following tests:

1. The bank's direct and indirect investment in and advances to the subsidiary equals five percent or more of the total equity capital of the parent bank. For the purposes of this test, the amount of direct and indirect investments and advances is either

a. the amount carried on the books of the parent bank or

b. the parent's proportionate share in the total equity capital of the subsidiary, whichever is greater.

2. The parent bank's proportional share (based on equity ownership) of the subsidiary's gross operating income or revenue amounts to 5 percent or more of the gross operating income or revenue of the consolidated parent bank.

3. The subsidiary's income or loss before income taxes amounts to 5 percent or more of the parent bank's income or loss before income taxes.

4. The subsidiary is, in turn, the parent of one or more subsidiaries that, when consolidated with the subsidiary, constitute a significant subsidiary as defined in one or more of the above tests.

Similarly Situated Bank

REGULATION CC, 12 CFR 229.2 (ee)

"A bank of similar size, located in the same community, and with similar check-handling activities as the paying bank or returning bank."

Sole Proprietorship

An unincorporated business owned by one individual.

Spec Housing

Residential dwellings built in anticipation, generally speculation, that sales will occur during or upon completion of construction.

Spread

The difference between the *bid rate* and the *offer rate* in an exchange rate quotation or an interest quotation. This difference is not identical with the profit margin because trades seldom buy and sell at their bid and offer rates at the same time. In another sense (for example, *Eurodollar* loans priced at a mark-up over LIBOR) *spread* means a *mark-up* over cost, and in this context the spread *is* identical with the profit margin.

Standby Contracts

Are optional forward contracts (see separate definition). For certain compensation (such as a fee or premium) the buyer of such a contract has acquired the right (or option) to sell to, or purchase from, another party some financial instrument at a stated price on a specified future date. For such compensation, the seller of the contract has become obligated to purchase or sell the financial instrument at the option of the buyer of the contract. Such contracts may relate to purchases or sales of securities, money market instruments, or futures contracts.

Standby Letter of Credit

A letter of credit, or similar arrangement that:

1. represents an obligation on the part of the issuing bank to a designated third party (the beneficiary), which is contingent upon the failure of the issuing bank's customer (the account party) to perform under the terms of the underlying contract with the beneficiary, or

2. obligates the bank to guarantee or stand as surety for the benefit of a third party to the extent permitted by law or regulation.

The underlying contract may entail either financial or nonfinancial undertakings of the account party with the beneficiary. The underlying contract may involve such things as the customer's payment of commercial paper, delivery of merchandise, completion of a construction contract, release of maritime liens, or repayment of the account party's obligations to the beneficiary. Under the terms of a standby letter, as a general rule, drafts will be drawn only when the underlying events fail to occur as intended. Standbys are included in the calculation of lending limits.

State Bank

REGULATION H, 12 CFR 208.1 (a)

"Any bank or trust company incorporated under a special or general law of a state or under a general law for the District of Columbia, any mutual savings bank (unless otherwise indicated), and any Morris Plan bank or other incorporated banking institution engaged in similar business."

Stock

A certificate documenting ownership in a corporate enterprise. For example, common stock represents equity ownership, and its holders' claims to income and assets are subordinated to creditors and preferred stockholders.

Stock Dividends

Distributions of additional shares to stockholders in proportion to the number of shares they own. Stock dividends provide shareholders additional ownership without reducing the total capital of the bank as occurs with the issuance of a cash dividend. Funds are transferred from undivided profits to the common stock account. Par value per share remains the same, while the number of shares issued and outstanding increases. Two-thirds of the shareholders must approve a stock dividend.

Stock Split

Division of an outstanding stock issue, which increases the number of outstanding shares. The intent is to reduce the price per share, thus making the stock more affordable for investors, and also to increase trading activity. (A stock split does not require the issuer to adjust its capital accounts as par value goes down and the number of shares increases. A majority of shareholders must approve a stock split.)

Subordinated Notes and Debentures

A form of debt issued by a bank or a consolidated subsidiary. When issued by a bank, a subordinated note or debenture is not insured by a federal agency, is subordinated to the claims of depositors, has an original weighted average maturity of seven years or more, and is not subject to federal interest rate limitations. Such debt shall be issued by a bank with the approval or under the rules and regulations of the appropriate federal bank supervisory agency.

When issued by a subsidiary, a note or debenture may or may not be explicitly subordinated to the deposits of the parent bank.

Subscription Right

A right present in some common stock issues, which gives the common stockholder the right to buy a proportionate amount of any new common stock issued by the company ahead of the general public.

Subsidiary

REGULATION K, 12 CFR 211.2 (p)

"An organization more than 50 percent of the voting shares of which is held directly or indirectly by the investor, or which is otherwise controlled or capable of being controlled by the investor or an affiliate of the investor."

REGULATION O, 12 CFR 215.2 (f)

"Subsidiary has the meaning given in 12 USC 1841(d), but does not include a subsidiary of a member bank."

Substandard Classification

Classification designating assets that are inadequately protected by collateral value, net worth of the borrower, and paying capacity of the obligor. Assets that are classified as such have well-defined weaknesses or weakness based upon objective facts that suggest the timely repayment or liquidation of the asset is problematic. Substandard assets are generally representative of assets that will result in the financial institution sustaining some loss if deficiencies are not corrected.

Sunset Provision

Provision in law, regulation, or contract that will terminate on a specific date.

Surplus

The "surplus" account is part of a bank's capital structure. Surplus is considered part of equity capital and may be paid in (sale price of stock less par value) or earned (transfers from undivided profits).

Suspense Accounts

Temporary holding accounts in which items are carried until they can be identified and their disposition to the proper account can be made. Such accounts may also be known as interoffice or clearing accounts.

Syndication

A syndication is a participation, usually involving shares in a single loan, in which several participants agree to enter into an extension that provides that, regardless of any event, each participant shall fund and be at risk only up to a specified dollar amount. In syndication, the participants agree to the terms of the participation prior to the execution of the final agreement, and the contract is executed by the obligor and by all the participants, although there is usually a lead institution organizing or managing the credit. Large commercial and industrial loans, large loans to finance companies, and large foreign loans may be handled through such syndicated participations.

Systemic Risk

Failure in a wire transfer or network environment of a system participant to settle its net debit position, which in turn will impact other institutions of expected funds and prevent those institutions from settling their net debit positions at the appointed time.

Also, systemic risk reflects risks in the financial services industry in which a number of financial institutions involved with certain types of business products, services, or transactions, or specifically, institutional performance, represent a risk to the industry.

T

Tangible Capital

The difference between a company's equity (GAAP basis) and the valuation of any allowed intangible assets (most often goodwill).

Tax Anticipation Note (TAN)

The most common type of municipal note sold in anticipation of tax receipts.

Taxpayer Identification Number (TIN)

Unique identification number assigned to each person or entity in the United States, that is, for people, a Social Security number.

Teller's Check

REGULATION CC, 12 CFR 229.2 (gg)

"A check provided to a customer of a bank or acquired from a bank for remittance purposes, that is drawn by the bank, and drawn on another bank or payable through or at a bank."

Teller's Station or Window

REGULATION P, 12 CFR 216.1 (f)

"A location in a banking office at which bank customers routinely conduct transactions with the bank which involve the exchange of funds, including a walk-up or drive-in teller's station or window."

Testamentary Trust

A trust established by the terms of a will.

Time Deposit

REGULATION D, 12 CFR 204.2 (c)

(1)(i) "A deposit that the depositor does not have a right and is not permitted to make withdrawals from within six days after the date of deposit unless the deposit is subject to an early withdrawal penalty of at least seven days' simple interest on amounts withdrawn within the first six days after the deposit [*See* footnote in the regulation for exceptions to this part of the definition]. A time deposit from which partial early withdrawals are permitted must impose additional early withdrawal penalties of at least seven days' simple interest on amounts withdrawn within six days after each partial withdrawal. If such additional early withdrawal penalties are not imposed, the account ceases to be a time deposit.

The account may become a savings deposit if it meets the requirements for a savings deposit; otherwise it becomes a transaction account. 'Time deposit' includes funds:

(A) payable on a specified date not less than seven days after the date of deposit;

(B) payable at the expiration of a specified time not less than seven days after the date of deposit;

(C) payable only upon written notice that is actually required to be given by the depositor not less than seven days prior to withdrawal;

(D) held in 'club' accounts (such as 'Christmas club' accounts and 'vacation club' accounts that are not maintained as 'savings deposits') that are deposited under written contracts providing that no withdrawal shall be made until a certain number of periodic deposits have been made during a period of not less than three months even though some of the deposits may be made within six days from the end of the period; or

(E) share certificates and certificates of indebtedness issued by credit unions, and certificate accounts and notice accounts issued by savings and loan associations.

(ii) a 'savings deposit;'

(iii) an 'International Banking Facility (IBF) time

deposit' meeting the requirements of Section 204.8(a)(2); and

(iv) borrowings, regardless of maturity, represented by a promissory note, an acknowledgement of advice, or similar obligation described in Section 204.2(a)(1)(vii) that is issued to, or any banker's acceptance (other than the type described in 12 USC 372) of the depository institution held by:

(A) any office located outside the United States of another depository institution or Edge or agreement corporation organized under the laws of the United States;

(B) any office located outside the United States of a foreign bank;

(C) a foreign national government, or an agency or instrumentality thereof, engaged principally in activities which are ordinarily performed in the United States by governmental entities;

(D) an international entity of which the United States is a member; or

(E) any other foreign, international, or supranational entity specifically designated by the Federal Reserve Board."

(2) A time deposit may be represented by a transferable or nontransferable, or a negotiable or nonnegotiable, certificate, instrument, passbook, or statement, or by book entry or otherwise.

Time Draft

A signed, written document in which the drawer instructs the drawee to pay a specified sum to a payee either on a definite date or at a specified time period after demand. Quite often, payee and drawer are the same.

Total Assets

REGULATION L, 12 CFR 212.2 (l)

"Assets measured on a consolidated basis as of the close of the organization's last fiscal year. The 'total assets' of a depository holding company include the total assets of all of its subsidiary affiliates, except that 'total assets' of a diversified savings and loan holding company, as defined in Section 408(a)(1)(F) of the National Housing Act (12 USC 1730a[a][F]), or of a bank holding company that is exempt from the prohibitions of Section 4 of the Bank Holding Company Act of 1956 pursuant to an order issued under Section 4(d) of that act (12 USC 1843[d]), means only the total assets of its depository institution affiliate. 'Total assets' of a United States branch or agency of a foreign commercial bank means the total assets of such branch or agency itself exclusive of the assets of the other offices of the foreign commercial bank."

Total Capital

The sum of primary and secondary capital.

Total Lease Obligation

REGULATION M, 12 CFR 213.2 (a) (17)

"Equals the total of

(i) the scheduled periodic payments under the lease,

(ii) any nonrefundable cash payment required of the lessee or agreed upon by the lessor and lessee or any trade-in allowance made at consummation, and

(iii) the estimated value of the leased property at the end of the lease term."

Trade Date

Date of actual transaction of the buying or selling of a security.

Transaction Account

A checking account or similar account from which transfers can be made to third parties. Demand deposit accounts, negotiable order of withdrawal (NOW) accounts, automatic transfer service (ATS) accounts, and credit union share draft accounts are examples of transaction accounts at banks and other depository institutions.

Both Regulation A and Regulation B use the same definition as Regulation D.

REGULATION D, 12 CFR 204.2 (e)

"A deposit or account from which the depositor or account holder is permitted to make transfers or withdrawals by negotiable or transferable instrument, payment order of withdrawal, telephonic transfer, or other similar device for the purpose of making payments or transfers to third persons or others or from which the depositor may make third-party payments at an automated teller machine (ATM) or a remote service unit, or other electronic device, including by debit card, but the term does not include savings deposits or accounts described in Section 204.2(d)(2) even though such accounts permit third-party transfers. 'Transaction account' includes:

(1) Demand deposits.

(2) Deposits or accounts on which the depository institution has reserved the right to require at least seven days' written notice prior to withdrawal or transfer of any funds in the account and that are subject to check, draft, negotiable order of withdrawal, share draft, or other similar item, except accounts described in Section 204.2(d)(2)(ii) (MMDAs), but including accounts authorized by 12 USC 1832(a) (NOW accounts).

(3) Deposits or accounts on which the depository institution has reserved the right to require at least seven days' written notice prior to withdrawal or transfer of any funds in the account and from which withdrawals may be made automatically through payment to the depository institution itself or through transfer of credit to a demand deposit or other account in order to cover checks or drafts drawn upon the institution or to maintain a specified balance in, or to make periodic transfers to such accounts, except accounts described in Section 204.2(d)(2), but including accounts authorized by 12 USC 371 a (automatic transfer accounts or ATS accounts).

(4) Deposits or accounts on which the depository institution has reserved the right to require at least seven days'

written notice prior to withdrawal or transfer of any funds in the account and under the terms of which, or by practice of the depository institution, the depositor is permitted or authorized to make more than three withdrawals per month or statement cycle (or similar period) of at least four weeks for purposes of transferring funds to another account of the depositor at the same institution (including a 'transaction account') or for making a payment to a third party by means of preauthorized transfer, or telephonic (including data transmission) agreement, order, or instructions, except accounts described in Section 204.2(d)(2). An account that authorizes more than three such withdrawals in a calendar month, or statement cycle (or similar period) of at least four weeks, is a 'transaction account' whether or not more than three such transfers are made during such period. A 'preauthorized transfer' includes any arrangement by the depository institution to pay a third party from the account of a depositor upon written or oral instruction (including an order received through an automated clearing house [ACH]), or any arrangement by a depository institution to pay a third party from the account of the depositor at a predetermined time or on a fixed schedule. Such an account is not a 'transaction account' by virtue of an arrangement that permits transfers for the purpose of repaying loans and associated expenses at the same depository institution (as originator or servicer) or that permits transfers of funds from this account to another account of the same depositor at the same institution or permits withdrawals (payments directly to the depositor) from the account when such transfers or withdrawals are made by telephone (via check mailed to the depositor) regardless of the number of such transfers or withdrawals.

(5) Deposits or accounts maintained in connection with an arrangement that permits the depositor to obtain credit directly or indirectly through the drawing of a negotiable or nonnegotiable check, draft, order, or instruction, or other similar device (including telephone or electronic order or instruction) on the issuing institution that can be used for the purpose of making payments or transfers to third persons or others, or to a deposit account of the depositor.

(6) All deposits other than time and savings deposits."

Transfer Item

REGULATION J, 12 CFR 210.26 (d)

"An item:

(1) sent by a transferor (other than a Reserve Bank) to a Reserve Bank for debit to the transferor's account at the Reserve Bank and for credit to a transferee;

(2) sent by a Reserve Bank to another Reserve Bank for credit to the latter or to any other transferee; or

(3) issued by a Reserve Bank at the request of a transferor for credit to a transferee."

Transfer Request

REGULATION J, 12 CFR 210.26 (e)

"A request by telephone that a Reserve Bank issue a transfer item."

Transferee

REGULATION J, 12 CFR 210.26 (f)

"A member bank, a Reserve Bank, or other institution that :

(1) maintains or, if authorized by the Reserve Bank, uses an account at a Reserve Bank and;

(2) is designated in a transfer item or request to receive the amount of the item or request."

Transferor

REGULATION J, 12 CFR 210.26 (g)

"A member bank, a Reserve Bank, or other institution that maintains or uses an account at a Reserve Bank and that is authorized by that Reserve Bank to send a transfer item or request to it."

Transferor's Account or Transferee's Account

REGULATION J, 12 CFR 210.26 (h)

"The account at its Reserve Bank maintained or used by the transferor or transferee, respectively."

Transferor's (or Transferee's) Reserve Bank

REGULATION J, 12 CFR 210.26 (i)

"The Reserve office at which the transferor or transferee, respectively, maintains or uses an account."

Traveler's Check

REGULATION CC, 12 CFR 229.2 (hh)

"An instrument for the payment of money that:

(1) Is drawn on or payable through or at a bank;

(2) Is designated on its face by the term 'traveler's check' or by any substantially similar term or is commonly known and marketed as a traveler's check by a corporation or bank that is an issuer of traveler's checks;

(3) Provides for a specimen signature of the purchaser to be completed at the time of purchase; and

(4) Provides for a countersignature of the purchaser to be completed at the time of negotiation."

Traveler's Letter of Credit

A letter of credit generally sold for cash and addressed by the bank to its correspondents, authorizing the correspondents to honor drafts drawn by the person named in the letter of credit in accordance with specified terms.

Treasury Securities

Interest-bearing obligations of the U.S. government issued by the Treasury as a means of borrowing money to meet government expenditures not covered by tax revenues. Marketable Treasury securities fall into three categories—bills, notes, and bonds. The Federal Reserve System holds more than $125 billion of these obligations, acquired through open market operations. Marketable Treasury obligations are currently issued in book-entry form only; that is, the purchaser receives a statement, rather than an engraved certificate.

Treasury Stock

Stock that a company, such as a bank, has issued and subsequently acquired, but that has not been retired or resold. As a general rule, treasury stock, whether carried at cost or at par value, is a deduction from a bank's total equity capital.

Troubled Debt Restructuring

Modification of credit extension original terms whereby the creditor grants concessions to a debtor, which normally would not be offered. Troubled debt restructuring occurs because the debtor's financial difficulties do not allow repayment according to terms.

Trustee

An individual or a trust institution that holds legal title to property for the benefit of someone else.

Trust Receipt

Receipt stating that the wholesale buyer has possession of collateral goods for the benefit of the floor plan lender; the borrower provides trust receipts to the bank to collateralize advances to purchase inventory. See also FLOOR PLAN LENDING.

Trustor

A person who creates a trust; it is a broad term that includes settlor, testator, grantor, and donor.

U

Unauthorized Electronic Fund Transfer

REGULATION E, 12 CFR 202.2 (l)

"An electronic fund transfer from a consumer's account initiated by a person other than the consumer without actual authority to initiate the transfer and from which the consumer receives no benefit. The term does not include any electronic fund transfer;

(1) initiated by a person who was furnished with the access device to the consumer's account by the consumer, unless the consumer has notified the financial institution involved that transfers by that person are no longer authorized,

(2) initiated with fraudulent intent by the consumer or any person acting in concert with the consumer, or

(3) that is initiated by the financial institution or its employee."

Undivided Profits

Unappropriated retained earnings.

Uniform Bank Performance Report (UBPR)

A report produced for each commercial bank in the United States, it is generated from a data base derived from public and nonpublic information sources. Information is presented in the form of ratios, percentages, and dollar amounts, primarily computed from the Reports of Condition and Income. Each UBPR also contains information for corresponding average data for peer groups and percentile rankings for most data.

United States Banks

This term covers both the U.S. and foreign branches of banks chartered and headquartered in the U.S. (including U.S. chartered banks owned by foreigners) but excluding U.S. branches and agencies of foreign banks. On the other hand, the term *banks in the U.S.* or *commercial banks in the U.S.* covers the U.S. offices of U.S. banks (including International Banking Facilities) and the U.S. branches and agencies of foreign banks but excludes the foreign branches of U.S. banks.

United States Resident

REGULATION D, 12 CFR 204.2 (s)

(1) "any individual residing (at the time of the transaction) in the United States;

(2) any corporation, partnership, association, or other entity organized in the United States ('domestic corporation'); and

(3) any branch or office located in the United States of any entity that is not organized in the United States."

Unit of General Local Government

REGULATION CC, 12 CFR 229.2 (kk)

"Any city, county, parish, town, township, village, or other general-purpose political subdivision of a state. The term does not include special-purpose units of government, such as school districts or water districts."

Unsecured Debt

Debt not backed by collateral.

V

Valuation Allowance

An account established against a specific asset category, or to recognize a specific liability, with the intent of absorbing some element of estimated loss.

Value at Consummation

PER REGULATION M, 12 CFR 213.2 (a) (18)

"Equals the cost to the lessor of the leased property including, if applicable, any increase or markup by the lessor prior to consummation."

Variable Rate

A variable rate agreement, as distinguished from a fixed rate agreement, calls for an interest rate that may fluctuate over the life of the loan. The rate is often tied to an index that reflects changes in market rates of interest. A fluctuation in the rate causes changes in either the payments or the length of the loan term. Limits are often placed on the degree to which the interest rate or the payments can vary.

Vault Cash

PER REGULATION D, 12 CFR 204.2 (k)

(1) "United States currency and coin owned and held by a depository institution that may, at any time, be used to satisfy depositor's claims.

(2) 'Vault Cash' includes United States currency and coin in transit to a Federal Reserve Bank or a correspondent depository institution for which the reporting depository insti-

tution has not yet received credit, and United States currency and coin in transit from a Federal Reserve Bank or a correspondent depository institution when the reporting depository institution's account at the Federal Reserve or correspondent bank has been charged for such shipment.

(3) Silver and gold coin and other currency and coin whose numismatic or bullion value is substantially in excess of face value is not vault cash for purposes of Regulation D."

Vested Interest

An immediate, fixed interest in real or personal property, although the right of possession and enjoyment may be postponed until some future date or until the happening of some event; this is distinguished from a contingent interest.

Vesting

An employee's right to receive a present or future pension benefit vests when it is no longer contingent upon his/her remaining in the service of the employer. Employee contributions are always fully vested; however, interest upon such contributions may not be vested, or may be paid at a specified rate, depending upon plan provisions. A vested benefit may be paid as a lump sum or, frequently, is paid as a deferred annuity upon retirement. Under ERISA, certain minimum vesting standards are prescribed.

Vostro Account

Used by a bank to describe a demand account maintained with it by a bank in a foreign country. The nostro account of one bank is the vostro account of the other bank.

W

Warehouse Receipt

An instrument that lists, and is a receipt for, goods or commodities deposited in the warehouse that issues the receipt. Such receipts may be negotiable or non-negotiable. A negotiable warehouse receipt is made to the "bearer" and a non-negotiable warehouse receipt specifies precisely to whom the goods shall be delivered. There are several alternatives for releasing goods held under warehouse receipts: The delivery of goods may be allowed only against cash payment or substitution of similar collateral. Some or all of the goods may be released against trust receipt without payment. A warehouseman may release a stipulated quantity of goods without a specific delivery order. Banks will accept a warehouse receipt as collateral for a loan only if the issuer of a receipt is a bonded warehouseman. The bank must have protected assurances for the genuineness of the receipt and the fact that the commodities pledged are fully available as listed on the warehouse receipt.

Warrants

Certificates given to stockholders or bondholders by an issuer that allows the holder to purchase a specific amount of its securities at a set price. A warrant can be sold to another investor if the holder chooses not to exercise the warrant.

Wholesale Funds

Uninsured deposits, brokered deposits, and funds borrowed in the financial markets.

Wire Transfer

REGULATION CC, 12 CFR 229.2 (ll)

"An unconditional order to a bank to pay a fixed or determinable amount of money to a beneficiary upon receipt or on a day stated in the order, that is transmitted by electronic or other means through the Federal Reserve Communications System, the New York Clearing House Interbank Payments System, other similar network, between banks, or on the books of a bank. 'Wire transfer' does not include an electronic fund transfer as defined in Section 902(f) of the Electronic Fund Transfer Act (15 USC 1693 a [6])."

Wrap-around Mortgage

A refinancing technique used in times of increasing or higher interest rates, in which the lender assumes payment of the existing mortgage and gives a new, increased mortgage to the borrower at a higher interest rate. As defined by its name, the new mortgage "wraps around" the original one. The increase amount is always second to the existing lien.

Y

Yield

Annual percentage rate of return on capital. The dividend or interest paid by a company expressed as a percentage of the current price.

SECTION II

A Glossary of Regulations

REGULATION A

(12 CRR 201)

Establishes rules under which Federal Reserve Banks may extend credit to depository institutions and others.

See	*Page*
Depository Institution	53

REGULATION B

(12 CFR 202)

Implements the Equal Credit Opportunity Act

Promotes the availability of credit to all creditworthy applicants without regard to race, color, religion, national origin, sex, marital status, or age (provided the applicant has the capacity to contract); to the fact that all or part of an applicant's income derives from a public assistance program; or to the fact that the applicant has in good faith exercised any right under the Consumer Protection Act. The regulation prohibits creditor practices that discriminate on the basis of any of these factors. The regulation also requires creditors to notify applicants of action taken on their applications; to report credit history in the names of both spouses on an account; to retain records of credit applications; and to collect information about the applicant's race and other personal characteristics in applications for certain dwelling-related loans.

REGULATION C
(12 CFR 203)

Implements the Home Mortgage Disclosure Act

It is intended to provide the public with loan data that can be used to help determine whether financial institutions are serving the housing needs of their communities and also to assist public officials in distributing public-sector investments so as to attract private investment to areas where it is needed.

REGULATION D

(12 CFR 204)

Relates to reserves that depository institutions are required to maintain for the purpose of facilitating the implementation of monetary policy by the Federal Reserve System.

REGULATION E

(12 CFR 205)

Implements the Electronic Fund Transfer Act

It establishes the basic rights, liabilities, and responsibilities of consumers who use electronic money transfer services and of financial institutions that offer these services.

REGULATION H

(12 CFR 208)

Outlines the eligibility requirements for a state bank or a mutual savings bank to be admitted to membership in the Federal Reserve System. It also outlines the application process and requirements of a state bank that becomes a member.

REGULATION J

(12 CFR 210)

Governs the collection of checks and other cash and noncash items, and the handling of returned checks by Federal Reserve Banks.

REGULATION K

(12 CFR 211)

Sets out rules governing the international and foreign activities of U.S. banking organizations, including procedures for establishing foreign branches and Edge corporations to engage in international banking and for investments in foreign organizations.

REGULATION L

(12 CFR 212)

The general purpose is to foster competition by generally prohibiting a management official of a depository institution or depository holding company from also serving as a management official of another depository institution or depository holding company if the two organizations are not affiliated and are very large and ocated in the same local area.

REGULATION M

(12 CFR 213)

Implements the consumer leasing portions of the Truth in Lending Act

The purpose of this regulation is to assure that lessees of personal property are given meaningful disclosures of lease terms, to delimit the ultimate liability of lessees in leasing personal property and to require meaningful and accurate disclosures of lease terms in advertising.

REGULATION O

(12 CFR 215)

Governs any extension of credit by a member bank to an executive officer, director, or principal shareholder of (1) the member bank, (2) a bank holding company of which the member bank is a subsidiary, and (3) any other subsidiary of that bank holding company. It also applies to any extension of credit by a member bank to (1) a company controlled by such a person and (2) a political party or campaign committee that benefits or is controlled by such a person. Regulation O also implements the reporting requirements of 12 USC 375 a concerning extensions of credit by a member bank to its executive officers and of 12 USC 1817(k) concerning extensions of credit by a member bank to its executive officers and principal shareholders.

REGULATION P

(12 CFR 216)

Establishes minimum standards for the installation, maintenance, and operation of security devices and procedures to discourage robberies, burglaries, and larcenies and to assist in the identification and apprehension of persons who commit such acts. It also establishes time limits for compliance and requires the submission of reports with the Federal Reserve.

REGULATION Q

(12 CFR 217)

Prohibits the payment of interest on demand deposits by member banks and other depository institutions and sets forth requirements concerning the advertisement of interest on deposits by member banks and these other institutions.

See	*Page*
Demand Deposit	48
Deposit	50
Foreign Bank	76
Interest	86

REGULATION S

(12 CFR 219)

Establishes the rates and conditions for reimbursement of reasonably necessary costs directly incurred by financial institutions in assembling or providing customer financial records to a government authority.

REGULATION U

(12 CFR 221)

Imposes credit restrictions upon banks (as defined by Regulation U) that extend credit for the purpose of buying or carrying margin stock if the credit is secured directly or indirectly by the margin stock.

REGULATION Z

(12 CFR 226)

Implements the Truth in Lending and Fair Credit Billing Acts

Its purpose is to promote the informed use of consumer credit by requiring disclosures about its terms and cost. Regulation Z also gives consumers the right to cancel certain credit transactions that involve a lien on a consumer's principal dwelling, regulates certain credit card practices, and provides a means for fair and timely resolution of credit billing disputes.

REGULATION AA

(12 CFR 227)

Defines unfair and deceptive acts or practices of banks in connection with extensions of credit to consumers.

REGULATION BB

(12 CFR 228)

Regulation issued to implement the Community Reinvestment Act (CRA) (12 USC 2901 et. seq.). The regulations under CRA authorize the Board of Governors to conduct examinations of state-chartered banks that are members of the Federal Reserve to assess performance per CRA. The regulation engages banks to help meet the credit needs of their local community or communities; and provides guidance on how the Board of Governors will assess state member bank performance in terms of satisfying their continuing and affirmative obligations to meet the credit needs of the delineated local community, including low- and moderate-income neighborhoods, consistent with safe and sound banking practices. The regulation further requires the Board to take in account the bank's performance per Regulation BB, in connection with certain applications.

See	*Page*
CRA	34

REGULATION CC

(12 CFR 229)

Implements the Expedited Funds Availability Act

Contains rules regarding the duty of banks to make funds deposited into accounts available for withdrawal, including both temporary and permanent availability schedules. Subpart B also contains rules regarding exceptions to the schedules, disclosure of funds-availability policies, payment of interest, liability of banks for failure to comply with Subpart B, and other matters. Subpart C contains rules to expedite the collection and return of checks by banks.

DEPARTMENT OF HOUSING AND URBAN DEVELOPMENT'S REGULATION

X

Implements the Real Estate Settlement Procedures Act

Its purpose is to promote more effective, advance disclosure to home buyers and sellers of settlement costs, to eliminate kickbacks or referral fees that tend to increase unnecessarily the costs of certain settlement services; to reduce the amounts home buyers are required to place in escrow accounts established to insure the payment of real estate taxes and insurance; and to reform and modernize local record keeping of land title information.

FEDERAL RESERVE ACT SECTION 23A

Outlines restrictions on transactions between member bank affiliates.

SECTION III

Acronyms

A

ABA	American Banker's Association*
ACH	Automated Clearinghouse*
AFT	Automated Funds Transfer
AICPA	American Institute of Certified Public Accountants
ALLL	Allowance for Loan and Lease Losses*
AMT	Alternative Minimum Tax
APR	Annual Percentage Rate*
ARM	Adjustable Rate Mortgage*
ATM	Automated Teller Machine*
ATS	Automated Transfer Service*

B

BA	Banker's Acceptance*
BAI	Bank Administration Institute*
BIF	Bank Insurance Fund
BIS	Bank for International Settlements*
BO	Branch Office*
BOP	Balance of Payments
BSA	Bank Secrecy Act*

* This term receives full treatment in the dictionary.

C

CA	Current Assets
CAMEL	Capital/Asset Quality/Management/ Earnings/Liquidity regulatory ratings
CBCT	Customer-Bank Communications Terminal (*See* ATM definition)
CCH	Commerce Clearing House
CD	Certificate of Deposit*
CEBA	Competitive Equality Banking Act of 1987
CEO	Chief Executive Officer
CFA	Chartered Financial Analyst
CFO	Chief Financial Officer
CFR	Code of Federal Regulations
CFTC	Commodities Futures Trading Commission
CMO	Collateralized Mortgage Obligation*
CMP	Civil Money Penalty *
CMV	Current Market Value
CRA	Community Reinvestment Act *
CRT	Cathode Ray Tube
CSVLI	Cash Surrender Value of Insurance
CUSIP	Committee on Uniform Securities Identification Number (Assigned to Securities)

D

D&B	Dunn & Bradstreet
DDA	Demand Deposit Accounts
DIDC	Depository Institutions Deregulation Committee
DIF	Deposit Insurance Fund
DPC	Debt Previously Contracted

E

E&O	Errors & Omissions
ECOA	Equal Credit Opportunity Act
EFT	Electronic Fund Transfer*
EFTS	Electronic Fund Transfer System*
EIC	Examiner-in-Charge*
EOM	End of Month
ERISA	Employee Retirement Income Security Act*
ESOP	Employee Stock Option Plan

F

FAC	Federal Advisory Council*
Fannie Mae (FNMA)	Federal National Mortgage Association*

FASB	Financial Accounting Standards Board
FCRA	Fair Credit Reporting Act
FCUA	Federal Credit Union Association
FDIC	Federal Deposit Insurance Corporation*
FED	Federal Reserve System*
FFIEC	Federal Financial Institutions Examination Council*
FHA	Federal Housing Authority*
FHLMC	Federal Home Loan Mortgage Corporation*
FIRREA	Financial Institutions Reform, Recovery, and Enforcement Act
FLB	Federal Land Banks*
FMV	Fair Market Value
FOIA	Freedom of Information Act
FOMC	Federal Open Market Committee*
FRB	Federal Reserve Bank; *also* Federal Reserve Board*
FTC	Federal Trade Commission
FX	Foreign Exchange*

G

GAAP	Generally Accepted Accounting Procedures
Ginnie Mae (GNMA)	Government National Mortgage Association
GO	General Obligation

H

HELOC	Home Equity Line of Credit*
HLT	Highly Leveraged Transaction*
HMDA	Home Mortgage Disclosure Act
HUD	Department of Housing and Urban Development

I

IBAA	Independent Bankers Association of America
IBF	International Banking Facility*
ICC	Interstate Commerce Commission
IMF	International Monetary Fund*
IRA	Individual Retirement Account
IRC	Internal Revenue Code
ITC	Investment Tax Credit

L

LBO	Leveraged Buyout (*See* Highly Leveraged Transaction definition)
LC	Letter of Credit*
LDC	Less Developed Country

LIBOR	London Interbank Offered Rate*
LPO	Loan Production Office

M

MIS	Management Information System
MMDA	Money Market Deposit Account
MO	Money Order
MSA	Metropolitan Statistical Area*
MSRB	Municipal Securities Rulemaking Board*

N

NASD	National Association of Securities Dealers
NA	National Association
NC	No Charge
NCUA	National Credit Union Administration
NOW account	Negotiable Order of Withdrawal Account*
NPV	Net Present Value
NSF	Non-sufficient Funds

O

OAPEC	Organization of Arab Petroleum Exporting Countries
OCC	Office of The Comptroller of the Currency
OD	Overdraft*
OLEM	Other Loans Especially Mentioned*
OREO	Other Real Estate Owned (*See* Real Estate Owned definition
OTC	Over the Counter Stock
OTS	Office of Thrift Supervision

P

P&L	Profit & Loss Statement
PIN	Personal Identification Number
PMI	Private Mortgage Insurance
POST	Point-of-Sale Terminal or Transfer

R

RAN	Revenue Anticipation Note
RAP	Regulatory Account Procedures
REIT	Real Estate Investment Trust*

REO	Real Estate Owned* (*See also* OREO)
RESPA	Real Estate Settlement Procedures Act* (*See* regulations directory)
ROA	Return on Assets*
ROE	Return on Equity*
RRP	Reverse Repurchase Agreement*
RSU	Remote Service Unit (*See* ATM definition)
RTC	Resolution Trust Corporation

S

S&P	Standard & Poor's
SAIF	Savings Association Insurance Fund
SBA	Small Business Administration
SBIC	Small Business Investment Corporation
SDRs	Special Drawing Rights
SEC	Securities and Exchange Commission*
SEP	Simplified Employee Pension Plan
SIPC	Securities Investor Protection Corporation
SMSA	Standard Metropolitan Statistical Area
SNAFU	Situation Normal, All Fouled Up

T

TA	Trade Acceptance
TAN	Tax Anticipation Note

TIL or TILA	Truth in Lending (Act) (*See* regulation directory)*
TIN	Taxpayer Identification Number*

U

UBPR	Uniform Bank Performance Report*
UCC	Uniform Commercial Code
USC	United States Code

V

VA	Veterans Administration

RESOURCE LIST

The following resources were utilized to prepare this dictionary.

Comptroller of the Currency. *Comptroller's Handbook for Compliance*. Updated Periodically.

_____. *Comptroller's Handbook for Consumer Examinations*. Updated Periodically.

_____. *Comptroller's Handbook for National Bank Examiners*. Updated Periodically.

_____. *Comptroller's Manual for National Banks*. Updated Periodically.

_____. *Comptroller's Handbook for National Trust Examiners.* Updated Periodically.

Downers, John, and Goodman, Jordan Elliot. *Dictionary of Finance and Investment Terms*. Woodbury, NY: BARRON's, 1985.

Federal Deposit Insurance Corporation. *DBS Manual of Examination Policies*. Updated Periodically.

Federal Financial Institutions Examination Council. *EDP Examination Handbook*. Updated Periodically.

Federal Home Loan Bank System. *FHLBS Regulatory Handbook—Thrift Activities*. Updated Periodically.

Federal Reserve System. *Bank Holding Company Supervision Manual.* Updated Periodically.

_____. *Federal Reserve Regulatory Service.* Updated Monthly. 4-Volume Set.

NCR. *Financial Terminology*. Dayton, Ohio: NCR, 1988.

SECTION IV

Index

A

B

C

D

E

F

G

H

I

J

L

M

N

S

T

U

V

W

Y